Living the Spirit of the Law
Instead of the Letter of the Law

The letter kills but the Spirit gives life. (2 Corinthians 3:6)

Ronald Higdon

Energion Publications
Gonzalez, FL
2025

Copyright 2025, Ronald W. Higdon

Scripture quotations marked ALTER are from *The Hebrew Bible: A Translation With Commentary* by Robert Alter, copyright 2019 by W. W. Norton & Company, New York.
Scripture quotations marked BARNSTONE are taken from *The New Covenant* by Willis Barnstone, copyright 2002 by The Berkley Publishing Group, New York.
Scripture quotations marked HART are taken from *The New Testament* by David Bentley Hart, copyright 2017 by Yale University Press, New Haven.
Scripture quotations marked HOLMAN are taken from *Holman Christian Standard Bible*, copyright 2004 by Holman Bible Publications, Nashville.
Scripture quotations marked NLT are taken from the *Holy Bible, New Living Translation*, copyright 1996, 2004, 2007, 2013 by Tyndale House Foundation. Used by permission of Tyndale House Publishers, Inc., Carol Stream, Illinois 60188. All rights reserved.
Scripture quotations marked MESSAGE are taken from *The Message*. Copyright 1993, 1994, 1995, 2000, 2001. Used by permission of NavPress Publishing Group.
Scripture quotations marked NJB are taken from *The New Jerusalem Bible*, copyright 1985 by Darton, Longman & Todd, Ltd. and Doubleday Dell Publishing Group Inc. All rights reserved.
Scripture quotations marked NRSV are taken from the *New Revised Standard Version*, copyright 1989 by the Division of Christian Education & the National Council of the Churches of Christ.
Scripture quotations marked RNT are taken from *The Restored New Testament* by Willis Barnstone, copyright 2009 by W. W. Norton & Company, New York.
Scripture quotations marked SCHONFIELD are taken from *The Original New Testament* by Hugh J. Schonfield, copyright 1998 by Element Books, Shaftesbury, Dorset.

Cover Design: Henry Neufeld

ISBN: 978-1-63199-943-7
eISBN: 978-1-63199-944-4

Energion Publications
1241 Conference Rd.
Cantonment, FL 32533

850-525-3916

pub@energion.com

Table of Contents

	Preface 1	
	Introduction..5	
1	Straining out Gnats and Swallowing Camels 13	
2	Not Destroying the Law but Completing It.............19	
3	A Shepherd – not a Wrangler 27	
4	Departing from Tradition.......................................37	
5	He Was not One of Us 43	
6	Do you understand what I have done?'....................51	
7	Is God too generous?..59	
8	Take Care How You Listen and How You Read......63	
9	Is a Mixture of Belief and Unbelief Enough? 75	
10	Doing Beautiful Things 81	
	Observations and Reflections at 90.........................89	
	Bibliography Of Quoted Sources............................95	

Preface

*"If you continue in My word,
 you really are my disciples.
You will know the truth,
 and the truth will set you free."*
John 8:31-32

Does it ever strike you as strange that the first "sign" in the Gospel of John that Jesus is the long-awaited Messiah is the turning of water into wine? (The other Gospels call such acts miracles rather than signs.) The very fact that Jesus and his disciples were invited to a wedding tells a lot. Later, the Pharisees will charge Jesus with being a glutton and a drunkard in shocking contrast to the ascetic life-style of John the baptizer (Mt. 11:19). I'm not suggesting that we see Jesus as a "party guy," simply as not someone who puts a damper on the attempts to celebrate life.

Jesus' ministry was life-affirming and, in this most "spiritual" of the Gospels, Jesus not only provides wine at a wedding but asserts: *"I have told you this so that my own joy may be in you and your joy may be complete"* (John 15:11). What he had just told them was the foundation for that joy: *"If you keep my commandments you will remain in my love just as I have kept my Father's commandments and remain in his love"* (Matthew 15:10). Jesus' "commandments" were of a different kind and degree and their dimensions were such that they were life-enhancing, not like the Pharisees' letter of the law that was deadening.

The reference has been lost but the essence of the account remains. A priest met Groucho Marx and greeted him with, "I want to thank you for all the joy and laughter you have brought to the world." Groucho responded with typical Marx humor: "And I want to thank you for all the judgment and gloom you have brought to the world!" Far too harsh and cynical but point made. When Jesus describes his followers, he calls them the salt of the earth and the light of the world (Matthew 5:13-16). However you interpret this, it speaks to adding zest and flavor as well as light that dispels the gloom and darkness that often envelops our lives. It speaks of people you like to have around you because they are not the balloon busters of rigid and joyless orthodoxy.

When Jesus talks about truth and freedom in John 8:32, he is talking about a special kind of truth and a special kind of freedom. Truth is not my own special kind of truth and freedom is not an "I did it my way" style of living. Truth is that which is provided by adopting Jesus' perspective on life, a particular way of seeing things, developing a mindset that goes to the deeper things of the law that includes intentions, motives, and emotions. The kind of freedom he talks about is something that frees life from the catalogue of lists and sets one's feet on the path as a follower of the Way.

The letter of the law turns out to be divisive, limiting, and much too narrow for the give and take of living in community. The Spirit of the law provides greater flexibility and removes one from always being on the defensive. Peter Tremayne has written a remarkable series of books featuring Sister Fidelma and life in seventh century Ireland. *Absolution by Murder* is Celtic history set in the year 664 during the famous Synod of Whitby. Advocates of both the Irish and Roman practices met to seek resolution of their differences. Some of the issues were their litanies, the date for Easter, and tonsure. Here are a few snapshots from the event:

> On the left side of the *sacrarium,* seated in rows, on dark oak benches, there had assembled all those who supported the rule of Columba. On the right side of the *sacrarium* were gathered those who argued for Rome.[1]

---

1   Peter Treymayne, *Absolution by Murder* (London: Headline Books, 1994), 45.

Bishop Colman took a step forward and traced the sign of the Cross in the air. Then he held up his hand and gave the blessing in the style of the church of Iona, using the first, third and fourth fingers to denote the Trinity as opposed to the Roman use of the thumb and first and second fingers. There was some murmuring from the ranks of the pro-Romans at this but Colman ignored it, asking a blessing in Greek, in which language the services of the church of Iona were usually said. The Deusdedit was helped forward and, in a soft whispering tone that underscored his apparent illness, he gave a blessing in the Roman style and Latin.[2]

"There has been much speculation as to the date of our Easter celebration," Cedd was saying. "Our gracious queen, Eanflaed, celebrates according to Rome. Our good king, Oswy, follows the teachings of Columba. Who is right and who is wrong? It can happen that the king has finished the fast and is keeping the Easter Sabbath while the queen and her attendants are still in Lent. This is a situation that sane men cannot countenance."

"True," called the pugnacious Wilfrid, not bothering to rise from his seat. "A situation rectified when you admit your error in your computation of Easter."[3]

The letter of the law is clearly illustrated in the physical separation of seating, the murmuring when the sign and words of blessing differ, and the sanity of the opposition is called into question over the dates for observing Easter. The spirit of the law is nowhere in sight.

We have a lot of unpacking to do and here is the way we plan to do it. Each chapter begins with a selection of Scripture followed by "Exegesis" (interpretation) of the passage. "Commentary," and then "Reflections," follow. "Worth Pondering" provides a variety of quotes and citings from works of fiction and non-fiction related to the subject of the chapter. The next section is titled "This and That" and includes observations that come from many directions. The final

---

2   Ibid, 54.
3   Ibid, 132.

section is "Anchors" where you will find Scripture references which provide a focus for helping maintain stability in times of tempest and turmoil. None of this is meant to be interpreted as "new rules," but as material for reflection, contemplation, and discussion. Life and faith are too full of mystery, paradox, ambiguity, complexity, and diversity to issue some narrow and inflexible rules for living.

Introduction

> *Our competence is from God, who has made us competent to be ministers of a new covenant, not of letter but of spirit; for the letter kills, but the Spirit gives life.* (2 Corinthians 3:5-6: NRSV).

> *My competence comes from God, who has qualified me to act as an administrator of a New Covenant not in letter but in spirit; for the letter kills, but the Spirit vitalizes.* (SCHONFIELD).

> *(God's new) plan wasn't written with ink on paper, with pages and pages of legal footnotes, killing your spirit. It's written with Spirit on spirit, his life on our lives!* (2 Corinthians 3:5-6: MESSAGE).

If it were a peripheral idea, it might not matter if it were the subject of occasional proclamation. However, it doesn't take much effort to make a case for its being central to the teaching of Jesus and the ministry of Paul. I am talking about the highly controversial text which is the basis for the title of this book, 2 Corinthians 3:5-6: *Our competence is from God, who has made us competent to be ministers of a new covenant, not of the letter but of the spirit; for the letter kills, but the Spirit gives life.*

I call it controversial because it is one of the major reasons the Pharisees were constantly leveling attacks at Jesus and it continues to be the unstated source of arguments, conflicts, and divisions in the Christian community. We need to begin with an analysis of the nature of the disagreements between those who advocate the letter of the law and those who attempt to live the spirit of the law.

EXEGESIS: 2 Corinthians 3:5-6

A better way to mark the divisions between the two great sections of Scripture is not "Old Testament" and "New Testament" but "Old Covenant" and "New Covenant." The old covenant made at the time of Moses stands in sharp contrast to the new covenant based on the death and resurrection of Jesus. In Paul's teaching about the Eucharist, he cites Jesus' words in offering the cup to his disciples at "The Last Supper": "*This...is the new covenant in my blood*" (1 Corinthians 11:25). Jesus announces this as the fulfilling of the prophet's promise in Jeremiah 31:31: "*The days are coming, says the Lord, when I will make a new covenant with the house of Israel and the house of Judah.*"

COMMENTARY

Many have suggested that a broader understanding of what Paul is writing about is revealed in his personal experience described in Romans seven and eight. His struggle to obey the written law brought frustration and despair; his life in the Spirit brought freedom, and peace as one adopted into God's family who could cry, "*Abba! Father!*" (Romans 8:15). In his experience, the new covenant brought a new relation with God and an entirely new dimension of living. His experience with the written law had been a dead end.

William Barclay (an author of practical, down-to-earth commentaries that provide easy and insightful readings) makes a case for the difference between a written document and the power of the life-giving Spirit. "The old covenant was a deadly thing. Why? It was so because it produced a legal relationship between (people) and God. In effect it said, 'If you wish to maintain your relationship with God, you must keep these laws, and if you break them your relationship is lost.'"[4]

---

[4] William Barclay, *The Letters to the Corinthians* (Philadelphia, The Westminster Press, 1956), 212.

If you believed you were keeping the law, you could congratulate yourself on your achievement. You were in good standing with God and you were proud of it. This misunderstanding of the keeping of the law is clearly illustrated in Jesus' charges against the Pharisees.

A story that provides some insight into interpreting 2 Corinthians 3:5-6 is Jesus' parable of two men at prayer. Since prayers were usually not offered silently, we overhear the praying of the two characters in the story (Luke 18: 9-14).

> *He also told this parable to some who trusted in themselves that they were righteous and regarded others with contempt: "Two men went up to the temple to pray, one a Pharisee and the other a tax collector. The Pharisee, standing by himself, was praying thus, 'God, I thank you that I am not like other people: thieves, rogues, adulterers, or even like this tax collector. I fast twice a week; I give a tenth of all my income.' But the tax collector, standing far off, would not even look up to heaven, but was beating his breast and saying, 'God, be merciful to me, a sinner!' I tell you, this man went down to his home justified rather than the other; for all who exalt themselves will be humbled, but all who humble themselves will be exalted." (NRSV).*

I can't resist inserting Eugene Peterson's treatment of the text in *The Message*. Here is his translation/interpretation:

> *He told his next story to some who were complacently pleased with themselves over their moral performance and looked down their noses at the common people: "Two men went up to the Temple to pray, one a Pharisee, the other a tax man. The Pharisee posed and prayed like this: 'Oh, God, I thank you that I am not like other people – robbers, crooks, adulterers, or, heaven forbid, like this tax man. I fast twice a week and tithe on all my income.' Meanwhile, the tax man, slumped in the shadows, his face in his hands, not daring to look up, said, 'God, give mercy. Forgive me, a sinner.'" Jesus commented, "This tax man, not the other, went home made right with God. If you walk around with your nose in the air, you're going to end up*

flat on your face, but if you're content to be simply yourself, you will become more of yourself."

EXEGESIS

"*Regarded others with contempt*" can literally be translated: "*Set all others at naught,*" meaning to "consider or treat as nothing." The tax collector "*standing afar off*" is contrasted with the Pharisee who "*stood,*" implying that he "struck an attitude ostentatiously where he could be seen." The tax collector's "*be merciful to me THE sinner,*" instead of "a sinner" speaks volumes. "The main point in the contrast lies in this article. The Pharisee thought of others as sinners. The publican thinks of himself alone as the sinner, not of others at all."[5]

COMMENTARY:

The reason the prayer of the Pharisee misses the mark is that he gets neither a true picture of himself or the tax collector. Malcolm Tolbert summarizes the problem like this:

> The problem with legalism is that it defines righteousness in such a way that it is attainable by men (sic). Having attained the standards by which they judge such matters, men are prone to fall into the sin or moral pride. There are two sides to this coin. On the one is erroneous judgment of the self; on the other is contempt for those who do not meet the standards.[6]

In Jesus' day, prayers could be offered at any time, but the times for public prayer at the Temple were daily at 9:00 a.m. and 3:00 p.m. Prayers were believed to be more effective when delivered at the Temple. The usual position in prayer was standing and, if you wanted to be seen, some spots were better than others. In the Sermon on the Mount (Matthew 6:6), Jesus advised going to a private place and

---

5 A. T. Robertson, *Word Pictures in the New Testament*, Vol. II. (Nashville: Broadman Press, 1930), 232-234.
6 *The Broadman Bible Commentary*, Vol. 9. (Nashville: Broadman Press, 1970), 141.

praying in secret. The Pharisees loved religion on parade. The object, of course, was to be seen. Jesus assured his listeners that those who prayed in secret were in the right place because God is one "*who sees in secret*" (Mt. 6:6). Prayer is never supposed to be for the benefit of an audience. Our only audience is God.

The Pharisee boasts about two matters that reveal what I like to call "excessive religion." The law required only one day of fasting a year (on the Day of Atonement); he fasted on Mondays and Thursdays of each week. The law required a tithe of certain agricultural products, but the Pharisee tithed on everything. When one lives by the law, it never hurts to put a little padding on things. Surely God has special blessings for those who go beyond the required minimum.

Many commentators point out that what the Pharisee delivered was not a prayer, but a monologue to himself on his religious achievements and his elevated position in the kingdom of righteousness. He didn't need to be made right with God; he was already right when he arrived at the place of prayer. He never asked for forgiveness or mercy because he didn't need either. He had achieved everything that God required to be in good standing.

Most of us are not able to capture the shock effect of Jesus' pronouncement at the conclusion of this parable: "*all who exalt themselves will be humbled, and all who humble themselves will be exalted.*" The one who goes home right with God is the one the Pharisee viewed as an unredeemed sinner (perhaps, even unredeemable). The Pharisee just went home; his condition remained unchanged. He was not right with God and he didn't know it. He was the one who was to be judged and he didn't know it. He was the one who had come short of God's requirements and he didn't know it. He left his time of prayer exactly as he had come: unaware of how much he needed the mercy and grace and forgiveness of God. In the parable, the one who received these gifts was the one who realized his need of them.

REFLECTIONS

The eye-catching title of an article in the Community Forum section of the *Courier-Journal* (5/7/25) reads: "I'm a U of L English major. It's a shame we don't value the humanities." Anna Williams makes a convincing case for these studies: "Literature has the power to promote empathy in people's lives as they read about others' experiences living. Writing has the power to be a transcendent vessel of information to better connect with others."

Williams later cites the 1989 movie, *The Dead Poet's Society*, and gives this quote from the teacher in the film, John Keating: "We read and write poetry because we are members of the human race. And the human race is filled with passion. And medicine, law, business, engineering – these are noble pursuits and necessary to sustain life. But poetry, beauty, romance, love – these are what we stay alive for."

The Christians' salt and light are to exemplify what we stay alive for. As in Jesus' ministry, we are to be those who contribute to the aliveness, joy, hope, and purpose of life – in the here and now. That "here and now" is the challenge that belongs to each of us in our particular place in this world.

A MOST SURPRISING THIS AND THAT

On the morning when I was ready to begin my final proofing and footnoting of this book, I was also completing my read of Peter Tremayne's *A Prayer for the Damned* (the fifth novel I had read in his Sister Fidelma series). I could not believe what I discovered and I am about to share. I thought about making it a Postscript following the Conclusion. However, because it speaks to the thesis of this book and exactly what I'm attempting to "prove" in these pages, I felt it should be up front. You may want to ask: How could a historical mystery set in A. D. 668 in Ireland have anything relevant to say to those of us in the twenty-first century? Well, just as Nathaniel wondered if anything good could come out of Nazareth, I invite you to "Come and see" (John 1:45-46). (Note: I am omitting certain names in order not to have to post a "spoiler alert.")

First, we need to set the stage for what is happening:

> _(His)_____ features were alight with fanatic zeal and Fidelma realized that he truly believed in his cause.
>
> "Thank God, it is not the *Penitentials* that rule this land, _____. At least you will now have to answer to the laws that do govern us," Fidelma said firmly as she stood up.
>
> _____ was undaunted. "You may shelter in your man-made rules, Sister Fidelma. Remember, you will, yourself, finally have to answer to the rules of Faith."
>
> "And what rules are they?" Fidelma asked sharply. "These *Penitentials*? Who set them down? Are they not also man-made?"
>
> "They are the law! The law of the Faith!" _____ replied vehemently.
>
> "I would have a care in your interpretation of the word 'law.'"
>
> "Christ said that he had come to fulfill the law, that the law was permanent and that people should obey it," grated _____.[7]

And now her argument:

> "And that law was Mosaic law, the ten commandments, not your *Penitentials* that have been devised to inflict suffering on mankind. Christ kept the commandments but he did not keep the law as made by men. Did he not set aside the understanding of his own people on issues like ritual cleansing, food laws and other matters – even the very understanding of the Sabbath day? Attend to your Scriptures and mark well, before you quote the words of Christ on law to me. If Scripture teaches anything, it

---

7 Peter Tremayne, *A Prayer for the Damned* (New York: St. Martin's Minotaur, 2006), 280-281.

is that it is not the appearance of law, the external appearance of purity and obedience, but its reality that should be obeyed. Christ's concern was for inner purity, for the ethic of the principle of truth rather than the ethic of rules for the sake of rules. You may claim to support the ethic of punishment of the transgressor in Cill Ria but I would hope that the true Faith teaches you the principle of charity."[8]

ANCHORS

Psalm 62:5-6: *Rest in God alone, my soul, for my hope comes from Him. He alone is my rock and my salvation, my stronghold: I will not be shaken… Trust in Him at all times, you people; pour out your hearts before Him. God is our refuge. HOLMAN).*

Romans 6:14: *Sin is no longer your master, for you are no longer subject to the law, which enslaves to sin. Instead, you are free by God's grace.* (NLT).

---

8   Ibid, 281.

Chapter 1:
Straining out Gnats and Swallowing Camels

Matthew 23:23-24

> *"Alas for you scribes and Pharisees, you hypocrites! You pay your tithe of mint and dill and cumin and have neglected the weightier matters of the Law – justice, mercy, and good faith! These you should have practiced; those not neglected. You blind guides, straining out gnats and swallowing camels!"* (NJB).

> *"You're hopeless, you religious scholars and Pharisees! Frauds! You keep meticulous account books, tithing on every nickel and dime you get, but on the meat of God's Law, things like fairness and compassion and commitment – the absolute basics! – you carelessly take it or leave it. Careful bookkeeping is commendable, but the basics are required. Do you have any idea how silly you look, writing a life story that's wrong from start to finish, nitpicking over commas and semicolons!'* (MESSAGE).

EXEGESIS

A detailed study of the Pharisees is beyond the scope of this book. However, a few relevant observations need to be made. Some Pharisees who become followers of Jesus are mentioned in Scripture (Nicodemus and Gamaliel). In Luke 13:31 some Pharisees warn Jesus to *"get away from here, for Herod wants to kill you"* (NRSV). References indicate that Pharisees were members of the Jerusalem congregation

(Acts 15:5). In Acts 23:6 Paul in his defense before a council in Rome calls out: *"Brothers, I am a Pharisee, a son of Pharisees."*

The Pharisees were a lay religious movement; the name probably means "separatist." There is no information about the origins of the group. They were committed to keeping the law as it was interpreted by the Scribes (scholars of the law). They produced a tradition that came to be known as the oral law. "This oral tradition came to be as important as the written law – perhaps even more so! The Pharisees therefore were devoted practically more to the legalistic traditions of the scribes than to the biblical Law."[9] When Jesus appears as a Rabbi who teaches with great personal authority and conducts an impressive healing ministry as he moves from place to place, the crowds keep increasing and his fame keeps spreading. One writer sees this as Jesus' major problem with the Pharisees: "The hostility of the Pharisees toward Jesus appears at the very beginning of the Gospel accounts, and seems to have arisen from the fear of the Pharisees that Jesus threatened their position as religious leaders."[10]

This text (Matthew 23:23-24) occurs in the context of seven woes concerning the Pharisaic Teachers (23:13-33). Most of these are concerned with the teaching of the Pharisees and scribes. The fourth woe is concerned with practice. "The opponents are chastised for paying so much attention to such trivial matters as the tithing of garden herbs…that they neglect the law's central demands: justice, mercy, and faith. It is possible that this trio of nonlegal obligations reflects Micah 6:8: *'And what does the Lord require of you but to do justice, and to love kindness (mercy), and to walk humbly with your God.'*"[11]

> The "weightier" matters do not refer to the "more difficult" or "harder" but to the "more central," "most decisive" or (as in NIV) "more important" versus "peripheral" or "trifling" ones. In

---

9   Watson E. Mills, ed., *The Mercer Dictionary of the Bible* (Macon: Mercer University Press, 1991), 681.
10 John L. McKenzie, *Dictionary of the Bible* (New York: Collier Books, 1965), 668.
11 Douglas R. A. Hare, *Matthew* (Louisville: John Knox Press, 1993), 269.

essence what Jesus accuses the teachers of the law and the Pharisees of is a massive distortion of God's will as revealed in Scripture.[12]

Barclay titles these two verses: "The Lost Sense of Proportion." Mint and dill and cumin are herbs of the kitchen garden, and would not be grown in any quantity. A man would have only a little patch of them in his garden; all these were used in cooking, and dill and cumin had medicinal uses. To tithe them would be to tithe an infinitesimally small crop, maybe not so much more that the produce of one plant. Only those who were superlatively meticulous would tithe the single plants of the kitchen garden. That is precisely what the Pharisees were like.[13]

COMMENTARY

> "The Talmud tells of the donkey of a certain Rabbi which had been so well trained as to refuse corn of which the tithes had not been taken."[14]

Although one of the above commentators in *The Expositors Bible* writes that the weightier matters of the law are not necessarily harder or more difficult, they are more central, I would suggest that they *are* more difficult because they have to do with what I term "relational theology." The two great commandments have to do with loving God and loving other people. Setting aside ten percent as an offering is much easier than having a proper relationship to God in faith (trust) and others in justice and mercy. One is simply math, the other deals with the complexities of life that cannot be reduced to percentages. With the weightier matters of the law, we get into the mind-bending and life-changing areas of forgiveness, reconciliation, and acceptance

---
12   *Expositor's Bible Commentary,* Vol. 8 (Grand Rapids: Zondervan, 1984), 480.
13   William Barclay, *The Gospel of Matthew,* Vol. 2 (Philadelphia: The Westminster Press, 1958), 324.
14   A. T. Robertson, *Word Pictures in the New Testament,* Vol I (Nashville: Broadman Press, 1930), 183.

of others without judgment. It's all the stuff the Sermon on the Mount talks about that makes Jesus' followers the salt of the earth and the light of the world.

REFLECTIONS

The problem I have always had with the letter of the law is that it is so divisive. It is either black or white. You're either in or you're out. You're either good or you're bad. You obey or you disobey. The contrasts can go to exhaustive lengths. Such literalism would have prevented Jesus from teaching without quoting different authorities, pronouncing forgiveness for people he healed, assuring the thief on the cross of a place in paradise, healing on the Sabbath, eating at the home of Levi and Zacchaeus, having a conversation with the woman at the well, teaching with Mary (the sister of Martha) seated at his feet, and welcoming women as supporting members of his traveling group.

The letter of the law is narrow and restrictive. The spirit of the law is full of compassion and inclusion. The letter of the law has its focus on "what we have always done"; the spirit of the law has its focus on new possibilities and dimensions of living. The letter of the law is heavy on judgment and the spirit of the law is heavy on grace.

WORTH PONDERING

> It was perhaps unusual for her to go to the girl's funeral – Lenox could think of no other woman of her class who would have done so – but Lady Jane simply was unusual…in her ability to do what she felt was right – even if it meant skipping lunch with a duchess to attend a maid's funeral – and maintaining her rarefied position at the same time. It was simply who she was. Her strength was in the integrity of her actions; she never compromised what she believed she ought to do.[15]

---

15   Charles Finch, *A Beautiful Blue Death* (New York: Minotaur Books, 2017), 124-125.

THIS AND THAT

Miriam Rothschild is one of David McCullough's "*Brave Companions.*" Her story is astounding from beginning to end. "In 1985, she was made a Fellow of the Royal Society, the highest honor in British Science. Yet Miriam Rothschild had little academic training of any kind – her family believed it would stifle the joy of learning."[16] Her interests and achievements are astounding. When anyone commented on her simple attire, she would always respond: "It's important to cut out the trivialities."[17]

In academia, that stifling is always a possibility. I know from experience. One of the worst Seminary classes I ever had (probably the worst) was taught by one of the best persons I have ever known. It was a required course in "missions" and was based on the seven-volume work by Kenneth Scott Latourette. The previous professor had made a detailed condensation; this served as the current professor's lecture notes. During three sessions a week, he carefully read these notes as those of us in the class attempted to take down our copy. These "lectures" were to form the basis for the final exam. The fifty-minute periods were tedious and tiring. We certainly got the details of the missionary endeavors but little else. We got the letter of missions but we certainly did not get the spirit of missions. We majored on trivialities – the grand sweep of things and the inspiring lives of those who led the way were nowhere in sight. We swallowed camels all semester.

A story I omitted in "*The Uncensored Story of a Minister's Life,*" I now provide. My home church as a teenager was a warm and caring place but I was unaware of how much fundamentalism overshadowed it. The minister's sermons were certainly biblically based but he was heavy on judgment and maintaining the letter of so much unwritten law that permeated Baptist life at the time. The list of the forbidden included: drinking, dancing, Sunday sports, movies, card playing

---

16   David McCullough, *Brave Companions* (New York: Simon & Schuster Paperbacks, 1992), 167.
17   Ibid.

(poker cast a shadow over all other card games) and a long list of temptations that came dressed in various ways.

A ritual at our house was Saturday night Rook. My sister and her husband usually made an appearance and my brother-in-law added much to the fun and laughter that always filled the evenings. For poor people, it was very inexpensive entertainment and a great family affair. One Sunday when the condemnation jar must have been getting about empty, our pastor added Rook cards to his list of prohibitions - they looked too much like regular cards. This was a time in my life when I tried too hard to live by the letter of the law and was much too much a fundamentalist in my own right. Our Rook nights were reduced in number and usually played with a little bit of guilt – certainly on my part.

About this time, rumors began to spread about the pastor's having a questionable relationship with a senior-high student. She was a member of the Louisville Baptist High School operated by our church. I also attended the school. The rumors turned to scandal with too much proof to ignore. A devastating turn of events followed that resulted in front page news and a court trial over property rights between those who supported the pastor and those who didn't. The result was the pastor's departure from the church and the city. My observation then to those who asked my opinion was simple: Just think how much better off he would have been at home playing Rook.

ANCHORS

> Psalm 100:2-5: *Serve the Lord with gladness; come before Him with joyful songs. Acknowledge that the Lord is God. He made us, and we are His – His people, the sheep of his pasture. Enter His gates with thanksgiving and His courts with praise. Give thanks to Him and praise His name. For the Lord is good, and His love is eternal. His faithfulness endures through all generations.* (HOLMAN).
>
> Romans 13:13: *There are three things that will endure – faith, hope, and love – and the greatest of these is love.* (NLT).

Chapter 2:
Not Destroying the Law but Completing It

Matthew 5:17

"Do not imagine that I have come to abolish the Law or the Prophets. In truth I have come not to abolish but to complete them." (NJB).

"Do not think that I came to destroy the Law and the prophets. I came not to destroy but to fulfill. For, amen, I tell you, until heaven and earth shall pass away, not a single iota or single serif must vanish from the Law, until all things come to pass. Whoever breaks one of the least of the commandments and teaches people to do so likewise shall be called least in the Kingdom of the heavens; but whoever performs and teaches it, this one shall be called great in the Kingdom of the heavens. For I tell you that, unless your uprightness surpasses that of the Scribes and Pharisees, you shall not enter the Kingdom of the heavens." (Matthew 5:17-20: HART)

"Don't suppose for a minute that I have come to demolish the Scriptures – either God's Law or the Prophets. I'm not here to demolish but to complete. I am going to put it all together, pull it all together in a vast panorama. God's Law is more real and lasting than the stars in the sky and the ground at your feet. Long after stars burn out and earth wears out, God's Law will be alive and working. Trivialize even the smallest item in God's Law and you will only have trivialized yourself. But take it seriously, show the way for others, and you will find honor in the kingdom. Unless you do far better than the Pharisees *in the manners of right living, you won't know the first thing about entering the kingdom."* (Matthew 5:17-20: MESSAGE)

EXEGESIS

It is to be remembered that the above paragraph is within the Sermon on the Mount (chapters five through seven in Matthew). Taken in isolation, it is much more difficult to understand and much of its meaning is lost in conjecture. This "sermon" is really the manual for those who have decided to follow Jesus. Reading the sermon in its entirety and then returning to read Matthew 5:17-20 provides perspective. Understanding the tone, the sense of direction – the overstory – is essential to any profitable exegesis.

"A single iota" or "a single serif" is the smallest Greek vowel or the smallest Hebrew letter; "a single serif" is the stroke above an abbreviated word or any small mark. "One suggestion is that the guilt of altering one of them is pronounced so great that if it were done the world would be destroyed."[18]

> This is perhaps the most difficult passage to be found anywhere in the Gospel. The difficulty pertains not only to ambiguity in certain key words such as "destroy" and "fulfill" but also to tensions between different clauses in the passage and between this passage and others in Matthew. The context presents Jesus as the God-authorized interpreter of the law. It must be assumed, then, that verses 17-20 are concerned with the relationship between Jesus and the law on the one hand and between his followers and the law on the other.[19]
>
> The formula *"Do not think that"* is repeated by Jesus in 10:34...The upshot of the introductory words is that they must be understood, not as the refutation of some well-entrenched and clearly defined position, but as a teaching device Jesus used

---

18 A. T. Robertson, *Word Pictures in the New Testament,* Vol. I, 43.
19 Douglas A. Hare, *Matthew,* 46.

to clarify certain aspects of the kingdom and of his own mission and to remove potential misunderstandings.

In verse 20, what Jesus demanded is the righteousness to which the law points, exemplified in the antitheses that follow.[20]

COMMENTARY

> "Matthew does not elaborate the meaning of this greater righteousness in an abstract essay, but explicates it by six concert examples that take up older materials and place them in a new interpretative structure."[21]

Jesus gives six examples of how he completes the law and makes it possible to have a righteousness that exceeds that of the Pharisees. Each of these goes beyond mere actions and probes beneath to desires, motives, and intentions. It speaks to the emotions that are churning within that signal destructive actions in the making (in the waiting room of our behaviors). As the new Moses, each of these is preceded by: *"You have heard that it was said…but I tell you…!"* Here is the authority of the Messiah voicing some of the dimensions of the new covenant of Isaiah.

Of course, one ought to refrain from murder, but also prohibited is anger and defaming language. Despising another and putting them down with damning language is a violation of this commandment. Even our offerings will be unacceptable if we are not right with our brother or sister. We are told to leave our gifts in front of the altar. *"First go and be reconciled with your brother, and then come and offer your gift"* (Mt. 5:24). The command not to murder, in its completed form, calls for reconciliation.

Adultery is on the list of prohibitions but expanded to include lust which is only held in check by lack of opportunity.

---

20 *The Expositor's Bible Commentary,* 147.
21 *The New Interpreter's Bible,* Vol. VIII (Nashville: Abingdon Press, 1995), 188.

The prohibition of divorce with nothing required but a written notice from the husband is updated by the new Moses. Scholars concur that there is nothing in the Torah that prohibits divorce. "The decision to divorce was strictly the prerogative of the husband, who did not have to go to court, but could simply make the decision himself in the presence of certified witnesses."[22] Jesus speaks against both divorce and remarriage; he raises questions about the exception clause *"except in the case of sexual immorality"* (Mt. 5:31). This issue is so complex that it would take a lifetime to plow through the interpretations, explanations, and applications of this complexion. Like everything else in Scripture, it must be understood in the culture of its time. Barclay maintains, "At that time the world was in danger of witnessing the break-up of marriage and the collapse of the home."[23]

Jesus condemns the taking of oaths which often involved using the name of God. He insists that the truth simply be spoken. The statement of the truth, without any shoring up by an oath, was all that is necessary. Some have taken this literally and have refused to take an oath as a witness in court. The completeness Jesus brought to this commandment was: truthfulness above all else – pure and simple.

When Jesus deals with one of the oldest laws in the world, *"an eye for an eye and a tooth for a tooth"* (the *Lex Talionis*), he throws it out the window. He teaches that life is certainly not about getting even (a never-ending proposition as current conflicts in our world illustrate). Jesus insists on turning the other cheek, giving away your coat, going the second mile, and being generous in helping others. We are not to return evil for evil but our business is to be those who are into positive, generous, and constructive living. Ours is not a measured goodness but a disposition of grace (we treat others just as God is treating us). This is one of the ways in which we become the salt of the earth and the light of the world. As with all these issues, much unpacking needs to be done in every particular situation – but

---

22   Ibid, 191.
23   William Barclay, *The Gospel of Matthew*, Vol I (Philadelphia: Westminster Press, 1958), 148.

the general principle remains the same. Repay evil with good. "No more resentment and retaliation."[24]

While there are no references in the Hebrew Scriptures to "*hate your enemy*," the command to "*love your neighbor*" (Lev. 19:18) clearly includes only other Israelites. Jesus completes this command by insisting that, in all personal relationships, love is the requirement for everyone. Jesus concludes this section of updated commands with: "*Be perfect, therefore, as your heavenly Father is perfect.*" The Greek word translated "perfect" is better translated as "be complete" or "be whole." God is complete in His love: no one is excluded as John 3:16 vividly presents. Jesus never met anyone who was beyond the boundaries of God's love. His inclusiveness is to be the model for our inclusive love.

REFLECTIONS

It remains true that many are so busy with the minutia that they miss the momentous. I remember as a preschooler, reading the story of a little pig who, after weeks of anticipation and saving his money, made his way to the circus that had just erected its tents on a large vacant lot outside the city. This was the day of many sideshows that beckoned one to attend before enjoying "the really big show." The little pig enjoyed several of these. When the time came to purchase his ticket for the show in the big tent, he discovered that he had spent all his money. I vividly recall the last picture in the book: a sad little pig making his way back home.

The story is almost like one of Jesus' parables: it makes us think and ask ourselves some of life's greatest questions: What are the big things in life that I want to make certain I don't miss? What is the most important thing I need to make certain is on my agenda today? If I were to write what I would like to see in my obituary, what would it include? (This is a practice recommended by many counselors – and not just as one approaches the end of life.) How can I establish priorities that will direct my life in a direction that has purpose and meaning? What are the big things in life that I don't want to miss?

---
24   Ibid, 163.

As Jesus sifted through the commandments and laws that dominated his culture, he always came back to the basics: the love of God and the love of neighbor. Even if that neighbor happens to be your enemy. Paul went so far as to conclude that there were only three things that had lasting qualities: faith, hope, and love. He quickly added, "*But the greatest of these is love*" (1 Corinthians 13:13). A big sidebar: In this famous love chapter, when Paul describes the kind of love he is talking about, he does not use adjectives, he uses verbs. He doesn't talk about how love feels; he talks about how love behaves.

WORTH PONDERING

Willis Barnstone's translation of the Gospels appeared under the title: "*The New Covenant*." The following information is taken from notes in that translation: Most of us have been accustomed to reading the traditional titles of the two major biblical divisions with the assumption that these have always been the givens. Not so. The Old Testament and the New Testament were the result of a mistranslation appearing in the Vulgate, the fourth-century translation attributed to Jerome. The exact translation of the Greek *kaine diatheke* in the Septuagint, 1 Corinthians 11:25, and Hebrews 8:8-13 is "*New Covenant*."[25] The clearest and most accurate titles for the two major divisions of Scripture are "The Old Covenant" and "The New Covenant." It sets the context for the understanding of Jesus' completion of the Law.

THIS AND THAT

The New York Times Magazine issue of May 4, 2025, carried a major illustrated article, "Our idea of happiness has become shallow. Let's go deep." Several quotes about the shallowness and ideas for going deeper, even though secular, echo the philosophy expressed in our text.

"Getting what you want in life – that's happiness bro," Saxon Ratliff tells his younger brother in the latest season of

---

25   Willis Barnstone, *The New Covenant* (New York: Riverhead Books, 2002), 9.

"The White Lotus" on HBO. Helpfully, he lists his essentials: sex, money, freedom, respect (in that order). …Once, happiness was understood as a communal project tied to justice and shared flourishing. But over time, it evolved from an expansive ideal into something individual and small.

When Thomas Jefferson and the other framers endorsed the pursuit of happiness, they were channeling a broad philosophical tradition. Happiness still bore the classical imprint – tied to justice and civic life…Happiness was *big*.

But not for long. Over the next century, its meaning began to contract. Once anchored in civic virtue and outward-facing ideals, happiness was increasingly treated as a personal feeling – a matter of mood, not meaning.

Is it possible that happiness stayed big, and it's only our way of talking about it that got small? Surely the old understanding, in which the pursuit of happiness is inseparable from shared commitments, hasn't gone anywhere.

ANCHORS

Psalm 58:11: *Then the people will say, "Yes, there is a reward for the righteous! There is a God who judges on earth!"* (HOLMAN).

Romans 1:16-17: *For I am not ashamed of this Good News about Christ. It is the power of God at work, saving everyone who believes – Jews first and also Gentiles. This Good News tells us how God makes us right in his sight. This is accomplished from start to finish by faith. As the Scriptures say, "It is through faith that a righteous person has life."* (NLT).

Chapter 3:
A Shepherd — not a Wrangler

John 10:11, 14

"I am the good shepherd. The good shepherd lays down his life for the sheep." (NJB).

"I am the good shepherd and I know my own and they know me." (BARNSTONE).

EXEGESIS

Sometimes a literal translation of some Greek words and their placement indicates the importance of the material being presented. John 10:1 begins with English introductions such as "*Very truly I tell you*" (NRSV), "*In all truth I tell you*" (NJB), or "*I assure you*" (NLT). David Bently Hart's translation of the Greek provides an important difference: "*Amen, amen, I tell you*." We usually think of an "Amen!" following something to which one adds a hearty endorsement. Jesus uses "Amen" as an announcement flag for something of prime importance, something not to be missed, something essential to the understanding of him, his ministry, and the Kingdom of God.

The context of John 10:11-15 is the contrast between good and bad shepherds. John also describes the relationship between the shepherd and his sheep. The good shepherd does not abandon his sheep when trouble (like wolves) comes but protects them even at the risk of his life. Sheep were dependent on the faithfulness of the shepherd for their survival; Jesus presents himself as the faithful shepherd who gives his life for his sheep.

The shepherd imagery is drawn from the Jewish Scriptures. Both Jer. 23:1-6 and Ezek. 34:1-34 present a denunciation of bad shepherds, God's promise to be shepherd and the coming Davidic king as good shepherd. John identifies Jesus as the fulfillment of these promises.[26]

The "*I am the good shepherd*" takes its place along with the many other "I am" sayings found in the Gospel of John: *"I am the bread of life"* (6:35); *"I am the light of the world"* (8:12); *"I am the resurrection and the life"* (11:25); *"I am the way, and the truth, and the life"* (14:6). The correlation with God's revelation of his name to Moses at the burning bush would be well-known to the first listeners of John's Gospel: "*Then Moses said to God, 'Suppose I go to the People of Israel and I tell them, 'The God of your fathers sent me to you'; and they ask me, 'What is his name?' What do I tell them?"* God said to Moses, "I-AM-WHO-I-AM. Tell the People of Israel 'I-AM sent me to you'"* (NJB). This will later prove to be the grounds for one of the major charges brought against Jesus as his "trial."

Even though the Hebrew title for the book of Psalms is "Book of Praises," there are more laments than praises in the book. This was the prayer book and the hymn book for the Jewish people. Voicing and singing our praises and our laments has been a common practice of cultures throughout history. We think especially of the "spirituals" that have come to us out of the slavery experience of African Americans. When we hear or sing them, we ought never to forget their origin.

One of my favorite commentaries for good ideas and summaries is the *Theological Bible Commentary*. The following quotations come from this book:

> In addition to its multifaceted focus on God, the Psalter provides an equally thick description of the human self, endowed with glory and honor yet also afflicted and vulnerable. The Psalter has been called the Bible's most introspective book, and appropriately so. To borrow language from John Calvin, the Psalter presents "an anatomy of all parts of the human soul," a profile of the human

---

26 Gail R. O'Day and David L. Peterson, eds., *Theological Bible Commentary* (Louisville: John Knox Press, 2009), 347.

self that plumbs the anguished depths of the heart while scaling the heights of intellectual and spiritual condition.[27]

In comparison to most biblical books, which bear some degree of cohesion or plot, the Psalter is a seeming hodgepodge of texts stemming from a variety of social settings and functions. In addition to its eclectic character, the Psalter's very medium – poetry – is by nature allusive and multivalent.[28]

REFLECTIONS

In a Peanut's cartoon, Linus is talking to Snoopy who sits on the top of his doghouse in front of a typewriter. Linus: "You know what Herman Melville said? He said, 'To produce a mighty book you must choose a mighty theme.'" Linus exits and Snoopy sits in a pondering position. In the last frame he is typing: "The Dog." He has found his mighty theme – himself.

Charles Schultz developed a group of characters who populated a children's world but addressed the major concerns and problems of the adult world. What will be the theme of the story I write about my life (written or unwritten)? What direction will I take, what path will I follow, which way will I go? A popular song of another generation gave one option: "I did it my way." The "me generation" (however you want to describe it) has used it as their theme song. A world of "selfies" will leave a plethora of photos of themselves in the center of every picture. Everyone else and everything thing else will be in the background. You won't be able to miss them; they are standing in the front row.

Psalm 23:1-3

The Lord is my shepherd; I shall not want. He maketh me to lie down in green pastures; he leadeth me beside the still waters. He restoreth my soul: he leadeth me in the paths of righteousness for his

---
27 Ibid, 177.
28 Ibid.

name's sake. Yea, though I walk through the valley of the shadow of death, I will fear no evil: for thou art with me; thy rod and thy staff they comfort me. Thou preparest a table before me in the presence of mine enemies: thou anointest my head with oil; my cup runneth over. Surely goodness and mercy shall follow me all the days of my life: and I will dwell in the house of the Lord for ever (KJV).

EXEGESIS

Called by many "the world's favorite psalm," it is probably the best-known chapter in the Bible, even to people who are not regular Bible readers. It is often heard at weddings and at funerals. The KJV is the classic and traditional translation often used but with "you" and "your" substituted for "thou" and "thy." There is also the modernizing of "leadeth," "preparest," and "anointest" to "leads," "prepare," and "anoint." Hebrew is not easily translated into English because Hebrew words are so rich in description and possibility. Some modern translations give new insights into other possibilities.

Robert Alter has provided a modern three-volume extraordinary and highly-praised translation of the Hebrew Bible. Here is one of his comments: "Although '*He restoreth my soul*' is time-honored, the Hebrew *nefesh* does not mean 'soul' but 'life-breath' or 'life.' [29] The image is of someone who has almost stopped breathing and is revived, brought back to life." Some will be unhappy with his translation of the final verse: A*nd I shall dwell in the house of the Lord for many long days.* His reasoning: "This concluding phrase catches up the reference to *all the days of my life* in the preceding line. It does not mean 'forever'; the view point of the poem is in and of the here and now and is in no way eschatological."[30] I think there are reasons for the traditional reading; one does not have to agree with everything an author says to still find his work profitable and enlightening.

Here is the version you will find in the New Jerusalem Bible:

---

29   Robert Alter, *The Hebrew Bible*, Vol. 3 (New York: W. W. Norton Company, 2019.)
30   Ibid, 71.

A NEW TRANSLATION FOR A NEW DAY

Yahweh is my shepherd, I lack nothing.
   In grassy meadows he lets me lie.
   In tranquil streams he leads me
      to restore my spirit.
   He guides me in paths of saving justice
      as befits his name.
Even were I to walk in a ravine as dark as death
I should fear no danger, for you are at my side.
Your staff and your crook are there to soothe me.
You prepare a table for me
      under the eye of my enemies;
you anoint my head with oil;
      my cup brims over.
Kindness and faithful love pursue me
      every day of my life.
I make my home in the house of Yahweh
      For all time to come.

For me, the most significant change is that, instead of God's love and mercy (kindness and faithful covenant love) following me, they *pursue* me all the days of my life. This is not a tag-along but the pursuit of God's Spirit in the watching, caring, and seeking that is consistent in all of Scripture, culminating in Jesus the Anointed One (Messiah) who declared his purpose to be: *"I have come to seek and save the lost"* (Luke 19:10). The use of "Yahweh" for Lord or God is the Hebrew YHWH which is the primary Hebrew word in the New Testament. There were no vowels in the Hebrew text; writers have added what they believe is the best possibility. Hence: Yahweh.

WORTH PONDERING

G. M. Malliet has written an insightful, witty, entertaining, and instructive series of mysteries featuring the Anglican Priest, Max

Tudor. His faith is deep and rich; he does not hesitate to find wisdom in many places.

> Finally, he decided that there was joy in surrender, in living according to the Buddhist precepts, in not trying to game the system and force events to turn in a particular direction. That way, thought Max, lies madness. In the long run, mankind did its worst work, and told the most lies, when trying to justify its actions, to impose a certain outcome.
>
> *Thy will be done.*[31]

The pages of G. M. Malliet's books are rich in humor:

My thanks to *The Epistle Magazine* of St. Paul's Episcopal Church, Alexandra, Virginia (Lent/Easter edition), for this inspiration: "Remember that the Lord has spoken often through dreams. Who knows what God is saying to the person who appears to be sleeping."[32]

Genesis, the new book on AI, has many promising and frightening perspectives to offer about what is already beginning to shape the world. I wrote my comment: "The Frankenstein monster updated" in the column following this prediction by the authors about AI machines: "In time, we should expect that they will come to conclusions about history, the universe, the nature of humans, and the nature of intelligent machines – developing a rudimentary *self*-consciousness in the process."[33]

A word of warning and some solid advice about AI is provided by this quote from Tolstoy: "Without control over the direction, there is less regard for the destination." The authors' comment: "Wherever technology takes us, that is where, willy-nilly we would go. Or, has been observed before, 'A nation which does not shape events through

---

[31] G. M. Malliet, *The Haunted Season* (New York: Minotaur Books, 2015), 15.
[32] Ibid, ix.
[33] Henry A. Kissinger, Craig Mundie, and Eric Schmidt, *Genesis* (New York: Little, Brown and Company, 2024), 66.

its own sense of purpose eventually will be engulfed in events shaped by others.'"[34]

The teaching of Jesus always focused on the way, the direction, the path, perspectives, attitudes, walking and living in the truth, and remaining open to the guidance of the Spirit. My philosophy has always been: "I'm into input, not outcome. That, as always, is in God's hands." If we continue in the right direction we can be assured that God will take care of the destination.

THIS AND THAT

In Luke, the history of God's covenant people really gets underway after a lengthy genealogy where we are introduced to Abram and Sarai. Beginning in chapter twelve of Genesis, history comes alive with the people, places, and stories of the great pilgrimage of faith with God's instruction to Abram, "*Go forth…*" (all Genesis quotes from ALTER). There was no detailed travel plan provided through the Mesopotamian Camel Club. It appears that, in some way, God just pointed in a direction and said, "Go that way." After God's promise that Abram would be a blessing, we are told that *Abram went forth as the Lord had spoken to him*. Faith is always an action word and includes moving in some way in the direction God has indicated. Faith is always on the move in the way and path that lead to blessings, especially blessings for others.

The early believers were known as "Followers of the Way." This in response to the only invitation Jesus ever gave: "*Follow me.*" Psalm 23 is not the picture of a "cattle drive" or a "herding" as animals are forced to move ahead of those bringing up the rear with shouts and commands. "*He leads me*" is the picture of sheep following a shepherd who is moving ahead to make certain the way is open and safe for the progress of his flock. It is leadership and not "drivership." It is not a frantic pace set to cover the most ground each day, but the purposeful and leisurely pace set by the walking shepherd. It is not a mad dash but a steady movement in the right direction.

---

34   Ibid, 190.

God's leadership has always been one more of direction and purpose than advance detailed directions. Psalm 86:11 sets the parameters for the faith journey: *Teach me, O Lord, your way. I would walk in Your truth* (all Psalm quotes from ALTER). *In Your light we shall see light* (Psalm 36:11) and *Send forth your light and Your truth. It is they that will guide me* (Psalm 43:3), give another picture of the kind of leadership God offers.

The New Covenant continues with these same images: *"I am the way and the truth and the life"* (John 14:6, HART); *"When that one comes, the Spirit of truth, he will guide you on the way to all truth"* (John 16:13). All of these verses point to something much more complex than a simple adherence to a list of rules. Following the Way, walking in truth, and being guided by light and truth indicate a journey that calls for more insight, flexibility, meditation, consultation, prayer, and decision making on our part along the way. It is indeed the journey of a pilgrim. It is a journey with all the challenges and detours that John Bunyan clearly outlines in his *Pilgrim's Progress*.

Jesus did not eliminate the rules and commandments, but he did put them in the context of a much larger dimension of living. I have found some rules that are extremely helpful. Like these insights from Jordan Peterson's *12 Rules for Life*.

> Aim small… Thus, you set the following goal: by the end of the day, I want things in my life to be a tiny bit better than they were this morning.[35]

> Attend completely and properly to what is right in front of you.[36]

> Pursue what is meaningful – not what is expedient.[37]

---
35 John Peterson, *!2 Rules for Life* (Toronto: Random House Canada, 2018), 95-96.
36 Ibid, 110.
37 Ibid, 161.

ANCHORS

My soul, praise the Lord, and do not forget his benefits. He forgives all your sin; He heals all your diseases. He redeems your life from the Pit; He crowns you with faithful love and compassion. He satisfies you with your youth is renewed like the eagle. Psalm 103:2-5. (NJB).

John 16:12-13: *"Oh, there is so much more I want to tell you, but you can't bear it now. When the Spirit of truth comes, he will guide you into all truth."* (NLT).

Chapter 4:
Departing from Tradition

Matthew 15:1-9.

Then Pharisees and scribes from Jerusalem came to Jesus and said, "Why do your disciples break away from the tradition of the elders? They eat without washing their hands." He answered, "And why do you break away from the commandment of God for the sake of tradition? For God said, 'Honor your father and your mother' and 'Anyone who curses his father or mother will be put to death.' But you say, 'If anyone says to his father or mother: Anything I might have used to help you is dedicated to God,' he is rid of his duty to father or mother. Hypocrites! How rightly Isaiah prophesied about you when he said: This people honors me with lip-service, while their hearts are far from me. Their reverence of me is worthless; the lessons they teach are nothing but human commandments." (NJB).

After that, Pharisees and religious scholars came to Jesus all the way from Jerusalem, criticizing, "Why do your disciples play fast and loose with the rules?" But Jesus put it right back on them. "Why do you use your rules to play fast and loose with God's commands? God clearly says, 'Respect your father and mother,' and, 'Anyone denouncing father or mother should be killed.' But you weasel around that by saying, 'Whoever wants to, can say to father and mother, What I owed to you I've given to God.' That can hardly be called respecting a parent. You cancel God's command by your rules. Frauds! Isaiah's prophecy of you hit the bull's eye:

These people make a big show of saying the right thing, but their heart isn't in it. They act like they're worshiping me, but they don't mean it. They just use me as a cover for teaching whatever suits their fancy. (MESSAGE)

EXEGESIS

The first thing to note in this encounter is that the Pharisees and scribes (experts in the law) represent an *official* delegation from Jerusalem. Jesus had already raised more than a few eyebrows when his disciples plucked and ate heads of grain on the Sabbath. This was immediately followed by Jesus' healing a man with a withered hand – presumably on the same Sabbath. These two episodes in chapter eleven are quickly followed by the unwashed hands controversy in chapter fifteen. This time we know for certain that a report will be carried back to the authorities at the Temple that this prophet from Nazareth must be stopped.

No evidence can be found in the Torah for the washing of hands before eating. But the oral tradition of the day required it, not for matters of hygiene, but to maintain ritual purity. It was all about purity laws and the issue of clean and unclean. Each day held many opportunities for contact with something (or someone) unclean. Washing the hands before eating, in a strictly spelled-out procedure, was necessary to maintain that ritual purity.

Mark deals with the issue more directly because his audience is basically gentile, not Jewish, as in the case of Matthew. In Mark 7:14-23 Jesus gives almost a graphic description of the digestive process. Following the teaching, Mark comments: *"Thus he declared all foods clean."* (NRSV). (The verse is in parenthesis and is considered a gloss by some translators.) Gentiles don't have to worry about the clean/unclean issue. When the question is about providing for the care of one's parents, Jesus, as always, puts people before religious tradition. Needs come first.

COMMENTARY

> If anything emerges with clarity from the Gospels, it is that Jesus lived within Judaism with true piety and at the same time, maintained freedom to differ radically with its strongest leaders and exponents.[38]

Matthew 15:1-9 describes another time when Jesus does not answer a question directly. He turns the question back on the questioners and asks why they use their rules to avoid the commands in Scripture instructing grown children to take care of their elderly parents. He charges the Pharisees and scribes with using rules to bypass a direct and weightier teaching of Scripture. Once again, they demonstrate their priorities: rules over people. Jesus always put people first. That is why he could heal on the Sabbath. That is why he could eat with sinners (wrong doers) and tax collectors. That is why his ministry was one of compassion, mercy, and forgiveness while theirs was one of judgment and exclusion.

REFLECTIONS

> Father Gorman: "I returned to this, my parish, and have tried to guide my people, the people of Araglin, along the true path ever since."
>
> "Surely there are many paths which lead to God?" interrupted Fidelma.
>
> "Not so," snapped Father Gorman. "Only those who follow the one path can hope to find God."
>
> "You have no doubt of that?"
>
> "I have no doubt for I am firm in my belief…We must remain true to our convictions."

---

38 *The Broadman Bible Commentary*, Vol 8 (Nashville: Broadman Press, 1969), 165.

"Is that so? My mentor, Morann of Tara, used to say that convictions are more dangerous enemies of the truth than outright lies."[39]

This scene from a book set in the seventh century in Ireland can be updated for my earlier years in church with the phrase, "Well, this is the way we've always done it." Father Gorman and too many in the churches I served make little place for the complexity and diversity that inhabit every human heart. We all haven't come from the same place, with the same experiences, and the same needs. The late Catherine Marshall (Peter Marshall's wife) gave this insightful observation: "God finds the secret stairway into every human heart." Another writer puts it like this: "On the spiritual path there are no one-size-fits-all itineraries."[40]

Traditions are established to provide identity, structure, and uniformity within a community. They initially are meant to be avenues for increasing faith and commitment. They can (and often do) become rigid ways of doing things that are requirements for orthodoxy. The requirement for handwashing Jesus' disciples ignored was not a simple and quick washing of the hands. It had to be done in a required way – moving in a "just so" way from the elbow to the hands. When the Pharisees got through with their handwashing directions, all sense of thanksgiving and the spiritual had been wrung right out of it. I'm certain the disciples expressed gratitude in some way appropriate to a group always on the move.

WORTH PONDERING

I have always wondered how a first-time listener to Jesus' teaching would report his experience to a friend who was not there. I have thought the dialogue might run something like this:

---

39 Peter Tremayne, *The Spider's Web* (London: Headline Books, 1997), 119-120.
40 Philip Goldberg, *Roadsigns on the Spiritual Path* (Boulder, CO.: Sentient Publications, 2006), 12.

"I heard Jesus from Nazareth teach today."

"What new rules does he have for us?"

"He really didn't give any new rules but he did tell some wonderful stories. Today I heard stories about a lost sheep, a lost coin, and a lost son. That last story is the one that moved me. He talked about a father who ran to meet his wayward son, and about the party he threw to celebrate his return. However, the ending of the story just didn't seem right. The faithful, dutiful son who worked for his father every day refuses to attend the party. The story ends with the sounds of music and dancing coming from the inside and the father pleading with his model son to join in welcoming his brother back home. I'm still trying to figure out how we are supposed to understand that story."

Although not a parable, many are still struggling to understand exactly what the writer of John 1 was saying in what we know as verses fourteen, sixteen, and seventeen:

And the word became flesh
  And lived among us.
  And we gazed on his glory,
  The glory of the only son born of the father,
  Who is filled with grace and truth.
From his bounty we have all received grace upon grace.
  And as the law was given through Moses,
  Grace and truth have come through Jesus the Galilean. (HART)

THIS AND THAT

A good rule for writing is probably also a good rule for living the spirit of the law: first, go with your heart, then you can go with your head.

One of the books I highly recommend is *The Hiding Place* by Corrie Ten Boom. (I recommend the 35th Anniversary Edition because of the Forward by Joni Erickson Tada and the Preface by Elizabeth

Sherrill.) The true story is set in 1941 Holland during the Nazi occupation. The Ten Boom family provides assistance and shelter for a large number of Jews whose very lives depend on escaping arrest due to their great sin – they are Jews! One of those who finds safety in the Ten Boom house is Meyer Mossel who had been cantor in the synagogue in Amsterdam. His name couldn't remain the same, so he was called Eusebius, after the fourth-century church father. "Changing Meyer's name was easy – at once he became 'Eusie.' But getting Eusie to eat non-kosher food was something else."

One day the paper announced that coupon number four was good for pork sausage. It was the first meat we'd had in weeks. Lovingly Betsie prepared the feast, saving every drop of fat for flavoring other foods later…Betsie placed a helping of sausage and potato before him. "Bon appetite." The tantalizing odor reached our meat-starved palates. Eusie wet his lips with his tongue. "Of course," he said, "there's a provision for this in the Talmud." He speared the meat with his fork, bit hungrily, and rolled his eyes heavenward in pure pleasure. "And I'm going to start hunting for it, too," he said, "just as soon as dinner's over."[41]

ANCHORS

>Psalm 31:24: *Be strong and courageous, all you who put your hope in the Lord.* (HOLMAN)
>Mark 1:27: *They were all amazed, and they kept on asking one another, "What is this? A new teaching – with authority!"* (NRSV).

---

41   Corrie Ten Boom, with Elizabeth and John Sherrill (Grand Rapids: Chosen Books, 2006), 118-119.

Chapter 5:
He Was not One of Us

Mark 9:38-40

> John said to him, "Master, we saw someone who is not of us driving out devils in your name, and, because he was not one of us, we tried to stop him." But Jesus said, "You must not stop him; no one who works a miracle in my name could soon afterwards speak evil of us. Anyone who is not against us is for us." (NJB).

EXEGESIS:

There is no doubt that John expected Jesus to congratulate him for attempting to stop a man who was "*driving out demons in your name.*" ("In the time of Jesus everyone believed in demons. Everyone believed that both mental and physical illness was caused by the malign influence of these evil spirits.")[42] This was an Old Testament problem noted in Numbers 11:26-30 that John may have had in mind. Instead, he receives a quick rebuke: "*Do not stop him.*" The key phrase in Peter's report is that the man *is* driving out devils and is doing it "*in your* name." The phrase "*in the name of Jesus*" has a prominent place in the life of the early church (Acts 3:6, 16; 4:7, 10, 30; James 5:14).

COMMENTARY

The disciples, like many groups today, want to feel special and the right to be exclusive in their association with "lesser" Christian believers. They have drawn lots of lines and have very strict boundaries. Some go the extreme: "They want to restrict salvation to their group

---

42 William Barclay, *The Gospel of Mark* (Philadelphia: The Westminster Press, 1956), 232.

alone."[43] All kinds of questions surface with this kind of attitude: Can any one group ever possess all the truth? Why shouldn't we rejoice when good is being done even by someone who is not one of us? Did Jesus ever call us to determine who was one of us and who wasn't? He indicates diversity in his statement: *"I have other sheep which are not from this fold"* (John 10:16, BARNSTONE).

John's question (the only one in the Gospel he is recorded as asking) interrupts Jesus' teaching about who is the greatest in the Kingdom. This teaching comes in response to his asking the disciples what they had been discussing out on the road. This discussion immediately follows Jesus telling his disciples about his coming death (Mark 9:30-32). This follows Jesus' taking Peter, James, and John to the top of a mountain and being transfigured before them. When they descended, they met a man who had brought his epileptic son to be healed by the disciples who were not on the mountain; they couldn't cast out the evil spirit (Mark 9:14-18). The "*we tried to stop him*" (Mark 9:38) appears to include *all* of the disciples. An irony not to be missed: here are disciples attempting to stop a man who was doing something they couldn't do!

Jesus certainly had the habit of eating with the wrong kind of people and welcoming those who were definitely "not one us." This is illustrated in his encounter with a man who was up a tree and out on a limb.

Luke 19:1-10

He entered Jericho and was passing through it. A man was there named Zacchaeus; he was a chief tax collector and was rich. He was trying to see who Jesus was, but on account of the crowd he could not, because he was short in stature. So he ran ahead and climbed a sycamore tree to see him, because he was to pass that way. When Jesus came to the place, he looked up and said to him, "Zacchaeus, hurry and come down, for I must stay at your house today." So he

---

43 *The New Interpreter's Bible,* Vol. VIII (Nashville: Abingdon Press, 1995), 639.

hurried down and was happy to welcome him. All who saw it began to grumble and said, "He has gone to be the guest of one who is a sinner." Zacchaeus stood there and said to the Lord, "Look, half of my possessions, Lord, I will give to the poor; and if I have defrauded anyone of anything, I will pay back four times as much." Then Jesus said to him, "Today salvation has come to this house, because he too is a son of Abraham. For the Son of Man came to seek and to save the lost." (Luke 19:1-10: NRSV).

EXEGESIS

"Jericho was an important trading point for balsam and other things and so Zacchaeus was the head of the tax collections in this region, a sort of commissioner of taxes who probably had other publicans serving under him." The tree he climbed was "the fig-mulberry and quite different from the sycamore tree…It was a wide-open tree with low branches so that Zacchaeus could easily climb into it."[44]

"When a person who unjustly acquired the property of another took the initiative in recognizing and confessing his wrong, he was required to return the property plus one-fifth of its value as compensation. Zacchaeus goes far beyond this."[45]

The expression *"to save the lost"* became widely used in the church, although "the lost" is a very rare term. It occurs here and in the parables of the sheep, the coin, and the father…The closing pronouncement (v. 10) makes it clear: Jesus' visit in Zacchaeus' house was not a delay or a detour on his journey to Jerusalem; this was and is the very purpose of the journey. *"The son of man came to seek and to save the lost."*[46]

---

44 A. T. Robertson, *Word Pictures in the New Testament*, Vol. II, 239.
45 *Broadman Bible Commentary*, Vol II, 147.
46 Fred Craddock, *Luke* (Louisville: John Knox Press, 1990), 220.

COMMENTARY

Working for Rome was enough to make one an outcast. Zacchaeus was despised not only for this connection but also because the tax system was heavy with misuse and corruption. The usual contract with tax collectors involved an amount set by the Roman government. Anything collected beyond that belonged to the collector. The system was not only open to abuse; it appeared to encourage it. His description of Zacchaeus as very rich made him a standout among most who were struggling to survive. Those who worked with him were probably his only "friends" and, even then, was probably not an ideal relationship.

Luke does not provide the context for Zacchaeus' desire to see Jesus, necessitating a mad dash for the mulberry tree. For one who enjoyed blending into the crowd, he became the stand out of the day. Although Jesus called Zacchaeus by name, we are not told how or why he knew it. We have no indication of a previous meeting; it seems that this meeting is a first-time encounter. Jesus shocks the crowd by announcing he intends to spend his time in Jericho at Zacchaeus' house. Of all the notable and worthy possibilities, Jesus selects from the bottom of the social scale and invites himself and his disciples to have lunch with a tax collector. This is a blatant affront to any Pharisees who happen to be in the crowd that day. You can be certain there were some. They made every effort to keep track of everything Jesus said and did. They were assembling a list of charges against him and this one would get five stars. You can't get any more "in your face" in disregarding religious and social expectations than this.

But the icing on the cake was yet to come. After Zacchaeus' amazing confession, Jesus pronounces this sinner, saved! *"Today salvation has come to this house."* Jesus' closing declaration only added fuel to a fire already blazing: *"This man is just as much a son of Abraham, a member of the covenant community, as any of you."* You can bet he didn't get a single "Amen!" that day. He only got an astonished crowd and a grateful and richly blessed "sinner."

REFLECTIONS

Luke is the only Gospel written by a non-Jew. This is part one of a two-part history (Luke and Acts): The Gospel from Jerusalem to Rome. The prologues to each of these books is unique as they describe the research and his relying on eye-witness accounts for his writing. The prologue in Acts lets us know it is a continuation of the story begun in the first book. When you think of the little out of the way place in which the Gospel began and read the last sentence in Acts, you are amazed at such overwhelming progress:

> *And Saul stayed two whole years in his own rented house and he welcomed all who came to him, preaching the kingdom of God and teaching about rabbi Jesus the Messiah, with open boldness and with no one hindering him.* (HART)

What is easily missed is that the last word in the original Greek text is *unhindered*.

The other amazing word for me in Luke's two-part work is found in Luke 23:42. The expansion of the gospel from Jerusalem to Rome demonstrates an inclusion beyond the imagination of the first Jewish disciples. This verse shatters all illusions of a gospel that excludes any who wish to enter. There are two criminals who are crucified with Jesus. As they hang on their individual crosses, one of them complains: *"Are you not the Messiah? Save yourself and us!"* But the other one reproved the first criminal and said, *"Do you not fear God, since you shared the same sentence? And we were justly punished, and are getting what we deserve, but he did nothing wrong."* Then he said, *"Jesus, remember me when you enter your kingdom."* (Luke 23:39-42, HART)

In the Gospels, Jesus is always addressed with some respectful title such as Teacher, Master, or Lord. No one ever calls Jesus by his first name! No one – except this criminal as he is dying on a cross. For me an even more significant aspect of his words comes from the notation in Hart's translation that the words *"when you enter your kingdom"* are not found in very early manuscripts. If we omit them, and read the more probable writing we have the criminal's last words:

"*Jesus, remember me!*" That's all! And Jesus' response reveals the new dimensions and inclusiveness of the New Covenant: "*Amen, I say to you, today you will be with me in paradise*" (23:43, HART).

Hidden from us in most translations is the way in which Jesus wanted to give added emphasis to what he was saying. He did so by using "Amen" at the *beginning* of his words instead of at the end. So he says to the criminal, "*Amen, I say to you…*" It is like a "Now hear this" important announcement on board a ship. Jesus proclaims the unthinkable: "This criminal is now one of us!"

WORTH PONDERING

Fidelma encounters a blind and deaf beggar who is in a far from presentable condition. This conversation follows:

> "Ignore him, sister," muttered Duban, "for he is cursed by God."
> "Can you not have him cleaned at least?" demanded Fidelma.
> "For what purpose?"
> "He is a human being."
> "The warrior grimaced sarcastically, 'Not that you would notice it.'"[47]

Our immediate response is that these are exactly the kind of people Jesus always noticed.

THIS AND THAT

In going through some old notes, I came across a sermon title: "My Future Ministry: With Commitment to the Christ of the Gospels." My opening was something I had forgotten and caught my attention with new affirmation:

In some places I am very broadminded and in others I am very narrow. I believe not in the Christ I can imagine or would like to find

---

[47] Peter Tremayne, *The Spider's Web*, 81.

acceptable: I believe in the Christ of the Gospels. Matthew, Mark, Luke, and John define, picture, and outline for me the Christ. That's where my basic information comes from.

I want to quote in full the section titled: "What do I believe in when I say I believe in the Christ of the Gospels? What do I see there?"

Here is my still current list of what I see:

I see a Christ who believed in the worth of every person (every person is created in the image of God).

I see a Christ who believed that every person is a recipient of God's love.

I see a Christ who was especially committed to the powerless.

I see a Christ who was especially concerned about the least of his brothers and sisters.

I see a Christ who was more concerned about the Spirit of the law than the letter of the law.

I see a Christ who modeled the way of greatness: the way of a servant.

I see a Christ who believed that what a person was would be evidenced in the way that person lived.

I see a Christ who constantly shocked the religious establishment of his day by the freedom, joy, and spontaneity with which he lived.

I see a Christ who shocked the orthodox by how unorthodox he was.

I see a Christ whose boundaries of the Kingdom were extended so that no one was excluded.

I see a Christ who was so winsome that even the little children gathered around him.

I see a Christ who so lived that at his crucifixion even a Roman solder could say, "*Truly, this man was the son of God.*" (Mark 15:49, HART).

I see a Christ who never gives up on me. I see a Christ who is committed to me.

I see a Christ who is worthy of my devotion and commitment.

ANCHORS

Psalm 108:3-5: *I will praise You, Lord, among the peoples; I will sing praises to You among the nations. For your faithful love is higher than the heavens; Your faithfulness reaches the clouds.* (HOLMAN).

Romans 1012-13. For there is no distinction between Jew and Greek; the same Lord is Lord of all and is generous to all who call on him. For "Everyone who calls on the name of the Lord will be saved." (NRSV).

Chapter 6:
Do you understand what I have done?"

John 13:4-5, 12-14

Jesus got up from the table, removed his outer garments and taking a towel, wrapped it around his waist; he them poured water into a basin and began to wash the disciples' feet and to wipe them with the towel he was wearing... When he had washed their feet and put on his outer garments again, he went back to the table. "Do you understand," he said, "what I have done to you? You call me Master and Lord, and rightly do; so I am. If I, then, the Lord and Master, have washed your feet, you must wash each other's feet. I have given you an example so that you may copy what I have done to you." (NJB).

EXEGESIS

There are other incidents and teachings that justify a wider meaning than seeing this as a call to wash each other's feet at special services. What Jesus was demonstrating was something much wider and deeper than merely adding another ordinance to accompany baptism and communion. When James and John make their request (Mark 10:35-37; in Matthew their mother makes the request) to sit one on his left and the other on his right in his kingdom, the other disciples are indignant with the two brothers. Jesus calls them all together and tells them:

"You know that among the gentiles the rulers lord it over them, and great men make their authority felt. Among you this is not to happen. No; anyone who want to become great among you must be

your servant, and anyone who wants to be first among you must be your slave, just as the Son of man came not to be served but to serve, and to give his life as a ransom for many." (Mark 10:42-45, NJB).

In Matthew 23:11 Jesus teaches: *"The greatest among you must be your servant. Anyone who raises himself up will be humbled, and anyone who humbles himself will be raised up"* (NJB). Jesus turns the world upside down when he declares that greatness wears the mantle of servant and the lofty are those who stoop to serve. When the Lord of glory kneels before his disciples and serves as a common slave, this is a demonstration of what it means to be a servant, of what it means to be truly great. This is not the letter of the law; it is the spirit of the law which always soars to another dimension.

COMMENTARY

Following Jesus' question, he does not so much give an answer, as to provide something for reflection and mediation: *"...if I your lord and rabbi washed your feet, you also ought to wash each other's feet. For I have given you an example for you to do as I have done to you"* (vs. 14 and 15, BARNSTONE). If you are following the letter of the law, the simple explanation and the easy way out is to take this as a command for a regular observing of a foot washing service where all believers participate.

On the way to what we term "The Last Supper," the disciples were discussing which one of them was the greatest. This may have been the reason not one of them volunteered to perform the foot washing task that was usually done by a servant. There was no servant present. The shocking revelation of the incident is that Jesus is the only servant present.

For many years in my pastorates, Monday would be the day for coffee and debriefing with fellow ministers (sorry: this was the day of very few women pastors). Questions arose like: "How many decisions did you have Sunday?" "How many baptisms did you have last year?" "How many people were present in your service Sunday?" This was all about the numbers game which appeared to be the bottom line in ministry and the indicator of how successful we were. The asker was usually one who was going "great-guns" (always seemed to me like a strange phrase to use for people in ministry) and wanted to do a little horn-tooting among his peers.

Jealousy, envy, and competition are no strangers to those in ministry. In the light of the Gospels, it is impossible to associate those words with ministry. I know how Jesus would respond to such attempts because I know how he responded to a question from Peter in John 21:21. This is the famous beach breakfast prepared by Jesus for his disciples sometime following his resurrection. Three times Jesus asks Peter if he loves him (no doubt referencing the three times Peter denies knowing Jesus). Peter gives three "*Yes, you know I love you*" answers. Each time Jesus commands, "*Then feed my sheep.*" He then gives a description of what will happen to Peter in the future. Jesus adds, "Follow me." Peter has his post-resurrection assignment.

Immediately (not in the text but implied by how quickly it happens), Peter turns and looks at another of the disciples and asks, "*What about him, Lord?*" Jesus rebukes him with: "*If I want him to stay behind till I come, what does it matter to you? You are to follow me.*" (John 24:20-22). Too many in ministry, and in life, appear to have missed reading this passage of Scripture. Our major concern is to stay busy with the tasks that belong to us. We are not to judge or compare ourselves with what others are doing. There are not many details about "Judgment Day," only that there will be one. It is what I call "The Day of Accountability," or better yet, "Rewards Day." Paul says it in a few words: "*For we will all strand before the judgment seat of God...So then, each of us will give an account of himself to God*" (Romans 14:10, 12, HOLMAN). Personal responsibility and personal accountability with no cross-references or comparisons with anyone else. Bottom line. Issue settled. The question, "But what about him?" will not be entertained; it is not on the agenda.

REFLECTIONS

The big question after reading this extraordinary episode in the life and ministry of Jesus is: Were the disciples ready to understand what Jesus had done? They were fresh from their arguing on the road which of them was the greatest. They were certain Jesus was about to make his big Messianic move and begin the establishment of an earthly kingdom to be inaugurated by the overthrow of Roman rule. (That is why James and John made their request for places of prominence in the new order of things.)

Some perspective is provided by Jesus' analysis of where the disciples were and of his remedy for their lack of understanding. *"I have many things to tell you but you cannot bear to hear them now. When the spirit of truth comes, he will guide you into the whole truth"* (John 16:12-13, HART). First: Jesus withheld much of what he wanted to teach them; he knew that their minds and hearts were not yet receptive. He promised that the Spirit would *guide* them into the whole truth. Jesus did not promise that suddenly the Spirit, in one great deluge, would dump the entire load of truth on them. The guidance into the whole truth would come gradually and would be timed to their openness to hear and understand. These two biblical principles cannot be overstressed.

In John 13, the disciples are reclining at a table they have no idea represents "The Last Supper" they will have with Jesus. They wouldn't have had room for such a thought anyway; they were too busy looking at each other and asking themselves, "How could any of these guys think they were the greatest?" Jesus breaks into this atmosphere of ambition and competition with a towel and a basin of water.

The disciples are simply caught up in that time of life where they are seeking to find their way and place in the world. We all need a time and the world needs young people to have a time when dreams, visions, and hopes fill the horizon. However, this is not forever to be. Nothing illustrates this better than the 1968 Mary Hopkin song, "Those Were the Days":

> Once upon a time there was a tavern
>> Where we used to raise a glass or two
>> Remember how we laughed away the hours
>> And think of all the great things we would do.
> Those were the days my friend
>> We thought they'd never end
>> We'd sing and dance forever and a day
>> We'd live the life we choose
>> We'd fight and never lose
>> For we were young and sure to have our way.

People used to seek wisdom from some aged wise person (the wise man on the hill), someone who had lived into some deeper understandings of faith and human existence. Unfortunately, in many ways it is now the youth culture that predominates. An example of this, which comes from many reliable sources, is that the contemporary worship that has now replaced traditional worship in most of the churches is nothing less that the youth retreat agendas that exploded not so long ago. Not all bad, of course, but not all tradition is bad either.

Things do look different when you are ninety. Ninety gives me a perspective I did not have earlier. I couldn't and shouldn't have had it anyway. I wasn't ready for it. We're not ready and our lives are not ready for the understandings that come only with the passing of time. Each period of our lives has appropriate emphases and agendas. Living at ninety as though we are twenty-five is both unrealistic and fool hearty. The same is true for living at twenty-five as though we are ninety. Knowing what time it is in our lives is the beginning of true wisdom.

WORTH PONDERING

The three key symbols of Jesus' pilgrimage among us are: a feeding-trough (incorrectly translated as "manger), a towel, and a cross. This is how *the word became flesh and lived among us* (John 1:14; HART). This turns upside down most of the current understandings of Messiah in Jesus' day. This turns upside down what it means to be a follower of the Way. This turns upside down what it means to be successful. This turns just about everything upside down, or as one writer contends, to turn things right side up. Jesus' question to his disciples after he washed their feet, "*Do you understand what I have done,*" can be placed right along the other unvoiced questions from the Gospels: "Do you understand the example I have set for you?"; "Do you understand why I said the first will be last and the last will be first?"; "Do you understand why I said the greatest of all will be the servant of all?"; "Do you understand how I said my followers were to be the salt of the earth and the light of the world?"; "Do you understand that it doesn't matter if you don't understand it all right now. Gradually, things will continue to unfold."

THIS AND THAT

> Something in his manner added to Max's impression of a man concerned with doing the right thing, but only if observed or certain to be lauded or rewarded for his selflessness. If unobserved, all bets would be off.[48]
>
> Now the dowager, pasting on a smile, braced herself to do good in a vague way. Hers was an all-encompassing brand of do-goodery, for she was the type to cut ribbons and make gushing little speeches of hope, flapping her scarves and jangling her bracelets and adjusting her rings, and generally trying to look beneficent, while her eyes rather desperately sought the whereabouts of the drinks tray.[49]
>
> "But I mustn't keep you," finished the dowager, and neatly side-stepping any attempts to get her actually help with the food preparation, she swanned her way into the dining room to mingle with the peons.[50]

---

48 G. M. Malliet, *The Haunted Season,* 61.
49 Ibid, 48.
50 Ibid, 49.

ANCHORS

Psalm 124:8: *Our help is in the name of the Lord, the Maker of heaven and earth.* (HOLMAN).

Matthew 20:26: *"It will not be so among you; but whoever wishes to be great among you must be your servant."* (NRSV).

Chapter 7:
Is God too generous?

Matthew 20: 9-11, 15

So those who were hired at about the eleventh hour came forward and received one denarius each. When the first came, they expected to get more but they too received one denarius each. They took it, but grumbled at the landowner…He answered one of them and said, "Why should you be envious because I am generous?" (NJB).

Those hired at five o'clock came up and were each given a dollar. When those who were hired first saw that, they assumed they would get far more. But they got the same, each of them one dollar. Taking the dollar, they groused angrily to the manager…He replied to the one speaking for the rest, "Friend, are you going to get stingy because I am generous?" (MESSAGE).

EXEGESIS

The setting of this parable was all too familiar to those who first heard it. The grape harvest at the end of September was a busy time - the rains were soon due to arrive accompanied by the loss of any grapes remaining on the vines. Day laborers (poor peasants who owned no property and the lowest class of workers) gathered in the market place (the equivalent of the labor exchange) to make themselves available for a day's work that began at 6:00 a.m. The desperation of their lives is reflected in the fact that some were still waiting at five o'clock to get work.[51]

The workday for the day laborer ran from six a.m. to six p.m. The owner of the vineyard makes several trips to the marketplace and hires workers at 6:00 a.m., 9:00 a.m., noon, 3:00 p.m., and 5:00 p.m. In "the Lord's Prayer," an alternate translation of Mt. 6:11 is sometimes provided

---
51 William Barclay, *The Gospel of Matthew*, Vol. 2, 245.

in a footnote. David Bentley Hart makes it his translation in the text. It reads: "*Give us today our bread for the day ahead.*" This reflects the literal day-to-day existence of those who needed to provide their wives with money at the end of each day in order that food could be purchased the next morning for that day. In the light of this situation, the owner's "generosity" is better understood for those who were hired at 5:00 p.m.

COMMENTARY

The first rule of interpreting Scripture is what I call the threefold rule: "Context! Context! Context!" Matthew was not written in chapters and verses. The modern division was made by Stephen Langton in 1228.[52] With a straight through reading, it is obvious that there should be no division between chapter 19 and chapter 20 of Matthew. In chapter 19, a rich young man comes to Jesus and asks, "*Master, what good thing must I do to possess eternal life?* (NJB). When he confesses that he has faithfully obeyed the great commandments, Jesus tells him that to be complete, he must sell his possessions, give the money to the poor, and follow him. Note: to no one else, including the wealthy, does Jesus ever make this demand. In this case, Jesus knew the man's wealth had become a barrier that had to be eliminated before he could become one of Jesus' followers. The young man sadly retreats and Jesus gives a brief lecture on the dangers of riches with his famous camel and eye of a needle illustration.

It is then that Peter speaks up and tells the Lord, "*Look we have left everything and followed you. What are we to have, then?*" (Matthew 19:27, NJB). After Jesus tells them, in essence, that their rewards will be beyond their imagination, he announces: "*Many who are the first will be last, and the last, first.*" It is then that he tells the parable of the laborers in the vineyard.

REFLECTIONS

It is true that in the parable all laborers received the same wage, but that is not its point. It points to the freedom and gen-

---

52 *The Broadman Bible Commentary*, Vol. 8, 193.

erosity of the *householder* in giving a full wage to laborers who had worked but one hour. It is a defense of the free grace of the gospel against the protests of those who stumble over this.[53]

In the telling of the story of the rich young man who comes to Jesus, only Mark adds: "*Then, looking at him, loved him* (10:21). Several such vivid details appear to be eye witness accounts. This is one of the reasons many believe Mark is based on the preaching of Peter. Two other exclusive details: only Mark says that Jesus was asleep on a cushion in the stern of the boat (4:37); in the story of Jesus and the children only Mark tells us he took the little ones in the crook of his arm (9:36; 10:16).

WORTH PONDERING

> This was one of things he hated most about coming off a bender: apologizing to everyone he'd offended. Sometimes, it went on for hours. Sometimes, he found out friends and relatives never wanted to talk to him again, and he prepared to lose a couple more.
>
> He told her what had happened. She broke in when he mentioned Alcoholics Anonymous.
>
> "I'm so proud of you for going," she said, her voice softening. "Why didn't you tell me?"
>
> "Because I fell off the wagon. I didn't want you to think I was a failure at that, too. Which, by the way, I did. Fall, I mean."
>
> "Then climb back on," she said. "There's no rule against that, is there?"[54]

THIS AND THAT

Then the girl turned and stared momentarily at him; or rather stared through him, because he felt that those deep, dark melancholy eyes did not really see him. But in that moment, Brother Augaire also saw the depth of the suffering in the girl's features. It was an expression

---

53 Ibid, 193
54 C. J. Box, *Back of Beyond* (New York: Minotaur Books, 2022), 71-72.

that was beyond grief. Its terrible beauty was hardened into a pale mask as if the girl had come to some fearful moment in her life when her very life's blood had frozen and never afterwards resumed its regular flow. Even the tears that had obviously been shed had long dried, but the fearsome abyss in her soul, the dark, cavernous well from which they had sprung, was still there. He could see it in those dark haunted eyes.

(A short time later): She was standing on the edge of the cliff, high above the crashing wave. Her pale arms were held up as if in supplication…The shout of "Stop!" died on his lips, as the girl seemed to throw herself outwards, as if taking a dive, her hands still held out before her as if in some entreaty.

"The girl is dead," Brother Augaire rebuked him.

"And by her own determination. The rule of our faith aside, suicide is a heinous crime under our native law: the ultimate form of kin-slaying which can neither be forgiven nor forgotten in a society such as ours that owes its very existence to the bond of kinship."

"But surely it must be understood," cried Brother Augaire.

"What is there to understand?"[55]

ANCHORS

> Psalm 13:5: *But I have trusted in Your faithful love; my heart will rejoice in Your deliverance. I will sing to the Lord because He has treated me generously.* (HOLMAN).

> Romans 8:31-32: *What can we say about such wonderful things as these? If God is for us, who can ever be against us? Since God did not spare even his own Son but gave him up for us all, won't God, who gave us Christ, also give us everything else?* (NLT).

---

55 Peter Tremayne, *A Prayer for the Damned*, 2, 4, 5-6.

Chapter 8:
Take Care How You Listen and How You Read

Mark 4:1-9

Again, he began to teach them by the lakeside, but such a huge crowd gathered round him that he got into a boat on the water and sat there. He taught them many things in parables, and in the course of his teaching he said to them, "Listen! Imagine a sower going out to sow. Now it happened that, as he sowed, some of the seed fell on the edge of the path, and the birds came and ate it up. Some seed fell on rocky ground where it found little soil and once it sprang up, because there was no depth of earth; and when the sun came up it was scorched and, not having any roots it withered away. Some seeds fell into thorns, and the thorns grew up and choked it, and it produced no crop. And some seeds fell into rich soil, grew tall and strong, and produced a good crop; the yield was thirty, sixty, even a hundredfold." And he said, "Anyone who has ears for listening should listen!" (NJB).

He went back to teaching by the sea. A crowd built up to such a great size that he had to get into an offshore boat, using the boat as a pulpit as the people pushed to the water's edge. He taught by using stories, many stories. "Listen. What do you make of this? A farmer planted seed. As he scattered the seed, some of it fell on the road and birds ate it. Some fell in the gravel; it sprouted quickly but didn't put down roots, so when the sun came up it withered just as quickly. Some fell in the weeds; as it came up, it was strangled among the weeds and nothing came of it. Some fell on good earth and came up with a flourish, producing a harvest exceeding his wildest dreams. Are you listening to this? Really listening?" (MESSAGE).

EXEGESIS

In each of the synoptic Gospels (Matthew, Mark, and Luke), the first parable is what is usually called "The Parable of the Sower." I prefer to give it the title of "The Listeners" or "The Ways We Listen." In the Greek text Jesus introduces the parable with the admonition "*Listen!*" The parable concludes with the same challenge: "*Anyone who has ears for listening should listen!*" Peterson ends his translation with the question: "*Are you listening to this? Really listening?*" Every parable is meant to leave us with homework – something that calls for reflection, self-judgment, meditation, commitment, and, usually, action.

When Jesus explains the parable to his disciples (Mk. 4:10-20), they understand it is not a lesson in better farming but something far more important: "*What the sower is sowing is the word*" (NJB). Jesus is the sower and the word is the gospel message. Whether or not the message takes root and produces fruit depends on the reception of the hearers. He cites four different types of soil (listeners) and four different results.

First, there is the unplowed ground. "The fields in Palestine were in the form of long narrow strips; these strips were divided by little grass paths; these paths were rights of way; the result was that they became beaten as hard as the pavement by the feet of those who used them."[56] The next kind of soil is that which is a thin layer over a shelf of limestone rock. The third kind of soil was full of thorns. The last kind of soil is deep, rich soil that provides the ideal growing conditions, resulting in an abundance of fruit. We now apply this to listeners.

The first group does not give the gospel a hearing because the tempter, the adversary, has already hardened their hearing against religious "nonsense." They don't even attempt to listen. The second group receives the good news but are taken aback when the gospel

---

56 William Barclay, *The Gospel of Mark*, 91.

does not produce a trouble-free life. They are looking for a philosophy that makes every day sunshine and rainbows. They stop listening. The third group also receives the word but the call of the world and the good "things" of life become too loud. It's all they can hear and they stop listening. The last group hears the good news with an open heart and life. It is just what they have been waiting to hear. It resounds in the depths of their souls and they know that at last they have met truth and life. They keep listening and keep producing the fruit of the Spirit (Gal. 5:22).

COMMENTARY

When Jesus interprets the parable for his disciples, he uses a phrase that has resulted in much discussion among biblical scholars: "*To you is granted the secret of the kingdom of God, but to those who are outside everything comes in parables*" (4:11, NJB). The most logical explanation of "the secret" I have found is its connection with what is known as the "Messianic Secret" in Mark. Jesus insists that those he heals not tell anyone that he is the Messiah. Too many popular ideas of the role of the Messiah (the liberation of Israel from Roman power) had nothing to do with his mission. Such announcements would bring a quick end to Jesus' ministry. It would be interpreted as one planning the overthrow of the government. "The secret of the kingdom of God must be associated with the identity of Jesus as the bearer of salvation…The disciples, who acknowledge him as Messiah and witness the transfiguration, will be silenced until after the passion" (Mk. 9:9).[57]

REFLECTIONS

> The parable of the sower invites us to reflect on the complexities of faith….Genuine growth in faith can be measured only by the developments in a person's life. Does faith endure prosperity as well as hardship? Does it yield fruit? Or is it like the tool we go

---

57   *The New Interpreters Bible*, Vol. VIII, 572.

looking for in an emergency, hoping we remember how it works? The self-help culture that sells people guaranteed quick fixes for all the difficulties of life often creates the expectation that faith should be the same – a comforting solution to the problems and pain of life. The interpretation given the parable of the sower reminds us that true discipleship does not provide such solutions.[58]

Luke 10:25-28

And look, a lawyer stood up to test him, saying, "Rabbi, what must I do to inherit eternal life?" And he said to him, "What is written in the law of the Torah? How do you read it?" The man answered and said, "You will love the Lord your God with all your heart, with all your soul, with all your strength and with all your mind, and you will love your neighbor as yourself." And Jesus said to him, "You answered right. Do this and you will live" (RNT).

Just then a religion scholar stood up with a question to test Jesus. "Teacher, what do I need to do to get eternal life?" He answered, "What's written in God's Law? How do you interpret it?" He said, "That you love the Lord your God with all your passion and prayer and muscle and intelligence – and that you love your neighbor as well as you do yourself." "Good answer!" said Jesus. "Do it and you'll live" (MESSAGE).

EXEGESIS

The parable that follows the scribe's question (*What must I do to inherit eternal life?*) and his response to Jesus' question (*How do you read it?*) are unique to Luke. A parallel conversation is found in Matthew 22:34-40 and Mark 12:28-34. In Matthew a Pharisee asks Jesus which is the greatest commandment and in Mark a scribe asks the question. In both accounts Jesus is the one who quotes the

---

58   Ibid, 574.

Scripture (Deuteronomy 19:18) about loving God and neighbor. One commentary suggests that the parable must be understood in its context; special attention must be paid to the questions of verses twenty-five: *"Master, what must I do to be saved?"* and twenty-nine: *"And who is my neighbor?"* This context also includes Jesus' application in verses thirty-six though thirty-seven: *"Which of the three do you think, proved himself neighbor to the man who fell into the bandits' hands?"* He replied, *"The one who showed pity toward him."* Jesus said to him, *"Go, and do the same yourself."*[59]

Another insightful contribution is the commentator's note about Jesus' affirmation of the scribe's answer. "Jesus affirms that the man answered correctly (*orthos:* "right," "properly," from which our word "orthodox" is derived). This does not mean that the inquirer has grasped the full meaning of the law, nor does it support the idea held by man that by keeping the law, as some kind of contract with God, a person can earn eternal life."[60]

COMMENTARY

Here, again, we have a vivid example of the difference between the letter of the law and the spirit of the law. Loving God and loving one's neighbor as yourself (most of the time someone in the neighborhood) can be accomplished with a sense of personal satisfaction. When Jesus asks the scribe how he reads, he is probing for much more than a literal interpretation of the texts. The spirit of the law is much more comprehensive and takes one into unfamiliar and challenging territory. Luke's Gospel is directed to the gentile world, as is illustrated in his going all the way back to Adam in giving Jesus' genealogy. This in contrast to Matthew's Gospel which is addressed largely to a Jewish audience; it begins Jesus' genealogy with Abraham (the father of the Jewish nation).

In most Bibles, divisions within chapters have titles that are not part of the text. The usual heading before Luke 10:25 is: "The

---

59 *The Expositors Bible Commentary,* Vol. 8, 942.
60 Ibid.

Parable of the Good Samaritan." Originally, parables were known by the first line in the story. *"There was a man who had two sons"* is the title of what we usually term "The Parable of the Prodigal Son," more accurately titled "The Parable of the Waiting Father." *"A Man was Going Down from Jerusalem to Jericho,"* and not "The Parable of the Good Samaritan" is the original title of this parable. If Jesus had announced this title for the story he is about to tell, he would not have gotten any further. There was nothing good that could be said about despised Samaritans.

Jesus' parable places the spirit of the law far above the letter of the law. It not only suggests that the Samaritan was to be included in the category of neighbor, it passes over the Priest and the Levite who "pass by on the other side" and makes the Samaritan the hero of the story. *"Which of these three, do you think, proved himself a neighbor to the man who fell into the bandits' hands?"* The scribe is forced to reply: *"The one who showed pity on him."* You will notice that he doesn't say, "The Samaritan." He couldn't bring himself to say that forbidden word.

When the scribe identifies the one who proved to be the neighbor, he uses words that speak to the spirit of the law: *"The one who showed pity towards him."* Now we are dealing with desires, motives, and intentions – matters of the heart and not just the head. Jesus never accused the Pharisees and scribes of failure to fulfill the letter of the law; he had much to say about their failure in areas of mercy and justice: *"Alas for you, scribes and Pharisees, you hypocrites! You pay your tithe of mint and dill and cumin and have neglected the weightier matters of the Law – justice, mercy, good faith!"* (Matthew 23:23). It is easier to be light-weight in matters of religion: just stick to the letter of the law. The weightier matters are much more difficult: they deal with who we are at the deepest level.

REFLECTIONS

How We Hear:

It is technically incorrect to plead, "The Bible says" because the Bible doesn't "say" anything. The Bible reads. We are the ones who determine what that reading says. A more correct statement is: "The Bible reads thusly and when I read it, I understand it to say…" In other words, a text of Scripture must be interpreted. There really is no uninterpreted reading of Scripture. Even when we read Scripture in a worship service, the listeners are hearing and interpreting it in the light of previous teachings, experiences, culture, age, and readings of this and other texts. We frequently come to Scripture with what we want to hear and too often that is what we hear.

Many have been led to believe that there is always a single meaning to any text of Scripture. To the contrary, there are multiple dimensions and levels of understanding to be gained from much of the biblical witness. Some of the rabbis taught that there were seventy different ways to read Scripture – one for every year of our lives. This is based on the expected lifespan of Psalm 90:10: *The days of our years are but seventy years, and if in great strength, eighty years…*(ALTER). Although not to be taken literally, its truth is that at different ages, different times in our lives, we read Scripture out of different needs, interests, and hopes.

An obvious indication of the different interpretations of Scripture is evidenced by the multiplicity of new translations that continue to appear. It is not that you will find contradictions in the different translations but you will find choices to use different meanings of the same Hebrew and Greek words with different shades of meaning that are found in the same words.

The proverb "let the text speak" is the ideal and should remain our priority. The bottom line is that we seek to understand the message the writer is trying to convey and we seek to discover what that meaning has to say to us in our time. We hear it in the context of the past and the context of the present.

How We Listen:

The Sound of Listening is a retreat journal by John Dear from Thomas Merton's Hermitage. A single excerpt hints at the richness and depth of what resulted from this retreat:

Brother Anthony is one of the main factory cooks. As he fixes the fire, I ask him if he has any advice. I think in terms of operating the wood-burning heater. He presumes I refer to my spiritual life.

"I have a Zen koan for you to ponder," he says, turning to me. "What is the sound of listening?"

He pauses and looks at me intently. The fire crackles.

The sound of listening?

"We are born into listening," he observes, "and we die into listening. Spend every minute here at the hermitage, like Merton, listening for the Spirit, letting the Spirit breathe in you and come alive in you. That's what prayer is about. You need no books, nothing at all. Just sit. Breathe in. Breathe out. And listen.

"It is that simple."[61]

With annual music events in Louisville like "Louder than Life" we can hardly imagine being able to hear anything with the noise of the culture turned up full volume. It often feels as though *everything* is louder than life – or at least louder than it ought to be. When I think of the sound of listening, the experience of the prophet Elijah immediately comes to mind. After the spectacular demonstration of God's fiery response on Mt. Carmel, followed by Elijah's running from the equally fiery wrath of Queen Jezebel, we find Elijah hiding in a cave in the wilderness. After a night's rest, *the word of the Lord comes to Elijah* (1 Kings 19:9) along with a command. Here is the episode:

> *And he said, "Go and stand on the mountain before the Lord, and, look, the Lord is about to pass over, with a great and strong wind tearing apart mountains and smashing rocks before the Lord. Not in the wind is the Lord. And after the wind an earthquake. Not in the earthquake is the Lord. And after the earthquake – fire. Not in the fire is the Lord. And after the fire a sound of minute stillness." And it happened, when Elijah heard, that he covered his face with his*

---

61 John Dear, *The Sound of Listening* (New York: Continuum, 1999), 55-56.

mantle and went out and stood at the entrance to the cave (1 Kings 19:11-13. ALTER*)*.

Robert Alter's translation is known for its unique capture of the Hebrew words, their arrangement, and flow. Other translations of *a sound of minute stillness* include: *a light murmuring sound* (NJB); *a soft whisper* (HOLMAN); *a gentle quiet whisper* (MESSAGE). Brother Andrew's advice to John Dear is right in line with Elijah's experience. When Jesus pronounced "blessed" those who had ears to hear, the implication is that many did not.

Apart from the spiritual dimension of listening, the practical benefits are immeasurable. In *The Lost Art of Listening* Michael Nichols and Martha Strauss have a single purpose: How learning to listen can improve relationships. Even the things we know, frequently need to be affirmed:

> Much of the conflict in our lives can be explained by one simple fact: People don't really listen to each other.[62] .
>
> We're bombarded with so much competing input vying for our attention – not only from the Internet, TV, and emails but now also from social media posts and Instagram – that our attention is fragmented. We like to think we're good at multitasking…We fool ourselves into thinking that we can do more than one thing at a time. The truth is that we just end up doing one thing after another poorly.[63]
>
> The simple art of listening isn't so simple.[64]
>
> The importance of listening cannot be overestimated. The gift of our attention and understanding makes other people feel validated and valued.[65]

---

62   Michael P. Nichols and Martha B. Straus, *The Lost Art of Listening,* Third Edition (New York: The Guilford Press, 2021), 1.
63   Ibid, 2.
64   Ibid.
65   Ibid, 6.

WORTH PONDERING

"What have I done wrong, and what can I do now to set things at least a little bit more right?"

"But your heart must be open to the terrible truth. You must be receptive to that which you do not want to hear."[66]

Despite him (Dupin) setting it out twice, (his mother) hadn't accepted his conclusions for a single minute, even at a rudimentary level, but had remained basically where she was. It was a technique – completely ignoring his information – which she had mastered perfectly. Anything she didn't want to hear she simply didn't hear. End of story.[67]

Doug Larson: Wisdom is the reward you get for a lifetime of listening when you'd have preferred to talk.[68]

Washington was accustomed to leading by listening…He was the most important person at the Constitutional Convention of 1787…His importance was a function of his presence, which lent an air of legitimacy to the proceedings…His silence during the debates was partially a function of his congenital reticence, but most the result of his role as president, whose job was to gavel the sessions to order, then listen as others spoke.[69]

THIS AND THAT

A 2015 report said one out of every four teens said that they were online "almost constantly." By 2022, that number had nearly doubled, to 46%. These "almost constantly" numbers are startling and may be the key to explaining the sudden collapse of adolescent mental health.[70]

---

66 Jordan B. Peterson, *12 Rules for Life*, 357.
67 M C. Beaton, *The Dead Ringer* (New York: Minotaur Books, 2020), 238.
68 Jason A. Merchey, *Wisdom* (Summerville, SC: Values of the Wise, 2022), 18.
69 Joseph J. Ellis, *His Excellency* (New York: Vintage Books, 2004), 175, 177.
70 Johanthan Haidt, *The Anxious Generation* (New York: Penguin Press, 2024), 34.

A 2015 report said that one out of every four teens said that they were online "almost constantly." As the MIT professor Sherry Turkle wrote in 2015 about life with smartphones, "We are forever elsewhere."[71]

Information doesn't do much to shape a developing brain. Play does. Experience, not information, is the key to emotional development. We might refer to smartphones and tablets in the hands of children as *experience blockers.*[72]

ANCHORS

Psalm 38:115: *I put my hope in You, Lord; You will answer, Lord my God.* (HOLMAN)

Luke 4:20: *He rolled up the scroll, handed it back to the attendant, and sat down. Everyone in the synagogue stared at him intently. The he said, "This Scripture has come true today before your very eyes."* (NLT).

---

71 Ibid, 34-35.
72 Ibid, 53-54.

Chapter 9:
Is a Mixture of Belief and Unbelief Enough?

Mark 9:24-28

"If you can do anything, have pity on us and help us." "If you can?" retorted Jesus. "Everything is possible for the one who has faith." At once the father of the boy cried out, "I have faith. Help my lack of faith!" And when Jesus saw that a crowd was gathering, he rebuked the unclean spirit. "Deaf and dumb spirit," he said, "I command you: come out of him and never enter him again." Then it threw the boy into violent convulsions and came out shouting, and the boy lay there so like a corpse that most of them said "He is dead." But Jesus took him by the hand and helped him up and he was able to stand. (NJB).

"If you can do anything, do it. Have a heart and help us!" Jesus said, "There are no 'ifs' among believers. Anything can happen." No sooner were the words out of his mouth than the father cried, "Then I believe. Help me with my doubts.!" Seeing that the crowd was forming fast, Jesus gave the vile spirit its marching orders: "Dumb and deaf spirit, I command you – Out of him and stay out!" Screaming and with much thrashing about, it left. The boy was pale as a corpse, so people started saying, "He's dead." But Jesus, taking his hand, raised him. The boy stood up. (MESSAGE).

EXEGESIS

Doing research in my Greek reference books brought new light to a simple word. The cry of the father is one of desperation which the

Greek text underscores. The word 'help' in 9:22 (*help us!*) is *boetheo*: "to run to the cry" of those in danger; it is the aorist imperative. Instant help is asked for. In 9:24 (*help my unbelief*), it is the present imperative. Continuous help is asked for. *'Be constantly helping my unbelief.'*

The word "unbelief," *apistia,* can be translated in this context by the expression "weakness of faith."[73] Peterson in his *Message* translation, captures the spirit of the military term Jesus uses in commanding the spirit to depart from the boy. This authority is in sharp contrast to the earlier inability of the nine disciples. Only in Mark does Jesus ask how long the boy has been suffering from this disease, showing his concern and sympathy. In this episode we see not only a demonstration of messianic power but the human side of a caring healer. Mark is also the only one who provides the setting: the disciples arguing with the scribes over their inability to perform the healing. A loss of face and a reflection on Jesus' ministry is the situation Jesus finds when he comes down from the mountain and the experience of Transfiguration.

If you read this account in Matthew 17:14-21 and Luke 9:37-43, you discover much shorter versions. "The story is so detailed in Mark that it has been suggested that this is one of the narratives Mark derived from Peter."[74] Not to be forgotten is that when the disciples are on an earlier mission: "*They cast out many devils, and anointed many sick people with oil and cured them*" (Mark 6:13). Many see this as the double issue of faith and power: "*I asked your disciples to drive it out and they were unable to*" (Mark 9:18). Jesus says that he has the power if only the father has the faith.

"*Everything is possible for one who has faith*" (Mark 9;24) probably does not mean that with faith one can do anything he chooses; but… that the man who has faith will set no limit for God's power."[75] This is a text that requires a great deal of unpacking to prevent it from becoming a simplistic and unrealistic attitude about the life of faith. Making it the only verse about personal faith, it ignores the complex-

---

73 Ibid.
74 *The Broadman Bible Commentary,* Vol. 8, 341.
75 Ibid, 341.

ities and complications that pervade our daily lives and ignores *thy kingdom come and thy will be done* of the Lord's Prayer. This is meant to provide the context and the frame of reference in which all our prayer requests are presented. It takes the focus off us and puts it on God's greater purposes. This puts us on the right road in our journey toward greater faith.

COMMENTARY

When the father uses the word "if" he applies it to Jesus' ability to heal his son. Jesus switches the application of the word to the father. It is not the ability of Jesus that is in question; the question is whether the father has faith in Jesus' power to heal his son. The father's cry, "*I believe, help my unbelief*" ((NRSV), suggests that even the intention of having faith or trust is enough to enable Jesus or God through Jesus to work the miracle.[76] The father did demonstrate a certain amount of faith in the very act of bringing his son to Jesus to be healed.

Was Thomas "Doubting Thomas"?

Nowhere in Scripture is the disciple Thomas referred to as doubting Thomas. That tag was attached because, not being present with the other disciples when Jesus made his appearance, he tells them, "*Unless, I see the mark of the nails in his hands and I* put *my finger into the place of the nails and I put my hand into his side, I shall not believe*" (John 20:25, BARNSTONE). I would call him "Seeking Thomas."

When Jesus receives news that his friend Lazarus is ill, he announces that he will return to the place where threats on his life have been announced. Thomas tells the other disciples: "*Let us also go so that we may die with him*" (John 11:16, BARNSTONE). I would call him "Brave Thomas."

When Jesus tells his disciples: "*In my father's house there are many rooms. If there were not so, would I have said to you that I go to prepare*

---

76   Gail R. O'Day and David L. Peterson, eds., *Theological Bible Commentary*, 318.

a place for you? And if I go to prepare a place for you, I will come again and take you to me so that where I am you may also be. And where I go you know the way," Thomas is the only one who voices what the other disciples surely are thinking: *"Lord, we do not know where you are going. How can we know the way?"* (John 14:2-5, BARNSTONE). I would call him "Honest Thomas."

And when Thomas finally meets the risen Lord, he does not find it necessary to do any touching, he simply makes the mountain-top confession in the Gospel of John: *"My lord and my God"* (John 20:28). I would call him "Believing Thomas."

A final reference to Thomas in John is found in 21:1-2: *"Thereafter Jesus again manifested himself to the disciples on the Sea of Tiberias; and this was the manner in which he manifested himself: Simon Peter, and Thomas…, and Nathanael…and the sons of Zebedee and two other disciples were together."* (HART). I would call him "Blessed Thomas."

Once again, the Gospel gives us much material for reflection, learning, and application.

REFLECTIONS

How we understand this episode depends on how we understand the Greek word *pisteuo* that occurs more than 240 times in the New Testament. It can be translated as "believe" or "trust." Proverbs 3:5 reads: *Trust in the Lord with all your heart* (ALTER) and reflects the consistent usage of any word that speaks of belief or faith in God. It is a relational word – not an intellectual word. In John 14, when translated as "believe" it certainly does not mean believing in a set of propositions about God and Jesus.

> The characteristic construction for saving faith is that wherein the verb *pisteuo* is followed by the preposition *eis*. It denotes a faith which, so to speak, takes a man (sic) out of himself and puts him into Christ…The man who believes in this sense abides in Christ

and Christ in him (John 15:4). Faith is not accepting certain things as true, but trusting a Person, and that Person is Christ.[77]

This is the reason I favor translations that deal with the Greek verb in a relational way – as trust. Examples: *"Do not let your heart be troubled: have faith in God and have faith in me"* (HART); *"Don't be troubled. You trust God, now trust in me"* (NLT); *"Don't let this throw you. You trust God, don't you? Trust me"* (MESSAGE).

The challenge presented by this text is not outdated. In our daily lives we are called to exercise faith and trust in God's ability. We are always seeking ways to grow in that faith and learn to live with the abiding confidence that God can take care of us in all situations – even those that throw us to the ground with the crowd counting us out. Our challenge is to cultivate whatever measure of faith we have and tend to its ongoing development. Bible study, prayer, and meditation are some of the best foundational building blocks in nourishing our faith.

WORTH PONDERING

"This Brother Solin was so certain that he represented the true way to your God and that all others dwelt in ignorance. I suppose you also argue that your way is the only way?"

Fidelma shook her head.

"I would not be that impertinent, Murgal. There are many paths to the same objective. We can be absolutely certain only about those things that we do not properly comprehend. To have a path through life made certain is the aspiration of most people in this unclear and uncertain existence. But certainty is often an illusion. We are born to doubt. Those who know nothing, doubt nothing."[78]

---

77   J. D. Douglas, ed., *The Illustrated Bible Dictionary*, Part 1 (Wheaton: Inter-Varsity Press, 1980), 497.
78   Peter Tremayne, *Valley of the Shadow* (London: Headline Books, 1998), 182-183.

THIS AND THAT

Asked about his religious beliefs, Albert Einstein responded:

We are in the position of a little child, entering a huge library, whose walls are covered to the ceiling with books in many different tongues. The child knows that someone must have written those books. It does not know who or how. It does not understand the languages in which they are written.

The child notes a definite plan in the arrangement of the books, a mystery order, which it does not comprehend, but only dimly suspects.

That, it seems to me, is the attitude of the human mind, even the greatest and the most cultured, toward God.

We see a universe marvelously arranged, obeying certain laws, but we understand the laws only dimly. Our limited minds cannot grasp the mysterious force that sways the constellations.[79]

ANCHORS

Psalm 69:6: *Do not let those who put their hope in you be disgraced because of me.* (HOLMAN).

Matthew 17:20: *Jesus said, "I assure you, even if you had faith as small as a mustard see you could say to this mountain, 'Move from here to there,' and it would move."* (NLT).

---

79 Henry A. Kissinger, Craig Mundie, Eric Schmidt, *Genesis*, p. 214.

Chapter 10:
Doing Beautiful Things

Mark 14-3-9

And when he was in Bethany, in the home of Simon the leper, reclining at the table, there came a woman who had an alabaster phial of pure, precious unguent of nard; breaking the alabaster phial, she poured it over his head.

But there were some who expressed indignation to one another: "Why has there been this waste of the unguent? For this unguent could be sold for more than three hundred denarii, and that given to the destitute." And they were angry at her. But Jesus said, "Leave her be; why do you subject her to abuse? She had done me a beautiful deed. For you always have the destitute with you, and you can do good to them whenever you wish, but you do not always have me. She did what she could; she has anointed my body, in anticipation for burial. Amen, I tell you, wherever the good tidings are proclaimed, in the whole world, what this woman did will also be told, as a memorial to her." (HART)

EXEGESIS

When John reports this, it is Judas who voices his indignation, "*not because he cared about the poor, but because he was a thief; he was in charge of the common fund and used to help himself to the contents*" (John 12:5). "Mark says that the other apostles '*had indignation among themselves,*' exchanging remarks or looks which told of their sympathy with Judas."[80] It is remarkable how quickly others join the judgment wagon as it rumbles past. No one questioned the motives

---
80 Kenneth S. Wuest, *Mark in the Greek New Testament*, 256.

of Judas or seemed to be aware of his pilfering on the side. This was probably unknown to them but one wonders how the writer of John secured this information.

The KJV reads: "*She hath wrought a good work on me.*" "The word 'good' here is not *agathos* which speaks of intrinsic goodness, but *kalos,* a goodness seen on the outside as it strikes the eye, a beautiful, pleasing goodness."[81] One wonders why the disciples did not have an eye for this beautiful goodness which was plainly evident to Jesus. This may be another illustration of his emphasis on the spirit of the law rather than the letter of the law (giving to the poor).

William Barclay titles this episode in Mark "Love's Extravagance." His commentaries are readable, down to earth, explorations into the text. He provides this picture of the setting:

> In Palestine people did not sit to eat. They reclined on low couches. They lay on the couch resting on the left elbow and using the right hand to take their food. So then anyone coming up to someone lying like this would stand well above them.[82]

Most estimates of the cost of this ointment suggest it was probably equal to a year's pay of the ordinary workman. It certainly was an extraordinary example of "Love's Extravagance."

Mark speaks of an unnamed "woman" who breaks in on the dinner at Simon's house. John gives the woman a name: "*Mary brought in a pound of very costly ointment, pure nard, and with it anointed the feet of Jesus, wiping them with her hair; the house was filled with the scent of the ointment*" (John 12:3). This Mary is the sister of Martha and Lazarus. In John eleven the story of Jesus receiving the message Lazarus' illness, the conversations with Mary and Martha after their brother has died, and the miraculous events at the tomb, provide the context that provides all the reasons for a demonstration of this beautiful deed of extravagant love.

---

81 Ibid.
82 William Barclay, *The Gospel of Mark,* 341.

COMMENTARY

Many things that are good may not necessarily be beautiful. When Jesus tells his followers in Matthew 5:16: "*Let your light shine before others, so that they may see your good works and give glory to your Father in heaven*" (NRSV), the word usually translated "good" is *kalos*. I maintain it should be translated as "beautiful" to reflect the kind of work illustrated by the unnamed woman in Mark. Too much radical goodness can be legalistic, harsh, judgmental, and simply overbearing. It reflects the kind of goodness found in the phrase, "Here comes Miss goody two-shoes." Most of us would privately pray, "Lord, save me from the people who parade excessive goodness." The perfect examples of goodness gone ugly are the Pharisees. The *kalos* kind of goodness is that which enables Jesus' followers to be the light of the world and the salt of the earth.

"In view of the occasion the action (of the woman) was especially fitting, for he was about to be put to death. Jesus would not interpret the anointing as referring to his royal dignity, but as an anticipation of his burial."[83] Jesus provided the interpretation of what the woman had done because he saw it as an anointment in anticipation of his death. As always, the interpretation is "in the eye of the beholder," and Jesus created the context for this to become a beautiful deed. His view was not one of extravagant wastefulness but of something to be remembered by future generations.

We are not to suppose that Mary anointed Jesus in recognition of his coming death. Like the other disciples, his death on a cross was unthinkable. What she did was in love and that deed and love were provided with dimensions of meaning she could not fathom. That is how our good works become the means of our being the light of the world. We give and act out of gratitude, thanksgiving, and love and God takes what we have done and makes it a beautiful work that shines light in our world and on his grace, mercy, and love in Jesus Christ, our Lord. We never know what will be seen in what we do or

---

83   *The Broadman Bible Commentary*, Vol. 8, 381.

what realities it will commemorate that are beyond our understanding or imagination.

A modern example of beautiful deeds of service is Mother Teresa. It is vividly captured by Malcolm Muggeridge's *Something Beautiful for God: the Classic Account of Mother Teresa's Journey into Compassion*. Quotes from his book need no commentary:

> To choose, as Mother Teresa did, to live in the slums of Calcutta, amidst all the dirt and disease and misery, signified a spirit so indomitable, a faith so intractable, a love so abounding, that I feel abashed.[84]

> When the Pope visited India, on leaving he presented her with his white ceremonial motor-car. She never so much as took a ride in it, but shrewdly organized a raffle with the car as the prize, thereby raising enough money to get her leper colony started.[85]

> With the various difficulties in the way of making our film about Mother Teresa and the Missionaries of Charity had all been dealt with, and we were in a position to go ahead, Mother Teresa said to me: "Now let us do something beautiful for God." I found the phrase enchanting, with a sparkle and gaiety very characteristic of her. It continued to echo in my mind, and when time came to choose a title for the film, *Something Beautiful for God* seemed the obvious one. Likewise for the book.[86]

---

[84] Malcolm Muggeridge, *Something Beautiful for God* (San Francisco: Harper & Row, 1971), 21.
[85] Ibid, 32.
[86] Ibid, 125.

Living by the Spirit of the Law

WORTH PONDERING

The story of the building of the Brooklyn Bridge is an incredible, amazing, and gripping story that David McCullough, in his *Brave Companions,* unfolds with his narrative history style that puts the reader right in the middle of everything.[87] It took fourteen years to build the bridge and it opened in 1883. The wisdom, perseverance, courage, and determination of those involved in the construction is a model for what is needed by all of us in whatever pursuits belong to us in this challenging world in which we live.

The miracle doesn't end with the construction of the bridge. The second miracle occurred in 1969 with the discovery of a thousand original blueprints and drawings. "The drawings by Washington Roebling, the commanding intellect, number some five hundred."[88] Although not in the same context, the following quotes remind me of what it is like in the work-a-day world to do something beautiful for God:

> In the last analysis, one comes to something in these drawings impossible to catalog, that has little or nothing to do with however much biographical or technical background one might compile. It is the incredible care and concentration you feel in even the least of the drawings, the pride, the obvious love – love for materials, love for elegance in design, love of mathematics, of line, of light and shadow, of majestic scale, and, yes, the love of drawing – this passion in combination with an overriding insistence on order, on quality, that we of this very different century must inevitably stand in awe before. You feel what these people felt for their work and you can't help but be drawn to them.[89]
>
> Frank Valentine likes to point out, "If there were 140 rivets in a connection, every rivet was drawn, and every one showing how the light would strike it." In drawing such as those of the caissons, each bolt and brace is shown; even the grain of the

---

87   David McCullough, *Brave Companions, 105-117.*
88   Ibid, 123.
89   Ibid.

wood is rendered, meticulously in watercolors. In part, but only in part, this can be explained by the fact that many who worked on the bridge were illiterate, or at least so far as reading plans, but as superb craftsmen they could build just about anything if it were pictured exactly as it was meant to look, exactly as it was supposed to be put together.[90]

An exhibition of sixty-five drawings painstakingly restored by hand (at a cost of $15,000) was held at the Whitney's downtown gallery in May 1976. "The first public display of the drawings was a huge success. The longer it was up, the greater the attendance, which is the reverse of the usual pattern. Remembering the response, Hupert says, 'No show we ever did had such an outpouring of affection, all for a bridge.'"[91]

THIS AND THAT

Is it possible to be salt and light at every time and every place? Is it possible to do something beautiful in one of the ugliest times in history? Another story from *The Hiding Place*:

> The evening's activity had to be kept brief because the city now had electricity only a short while each night, and candles had to be hoarded for emergencies. When the lamps flickered and dimmed, we would wind back down to the dining room where my bicycle was set up on its stand. One of us would climb onto it, and others taking chairs, and then while the rider pedaled furiously to make the headlight glow brighter, someone would pick up the chapter form the night before. We changed cyclist and reader often as legs or voices grew tired, reading our way through histories, novels, plays.[92]

---

90   Ibid.
91   Ibid, 121.
92   Corrie ten Boom, *The Hiding Place,* 124.

Being the light of the world is no easy matter! It may take a lot of pedaling when everything around is a night of blackness.

ANCHORS

Psalm 103:8, 10: *The Lord is compassionate and gracious, slow to anger and full of faithful love…He has not dealt with us as our sins deserve or repaid us according to our offenses.* (HOLMAN).

Matthew 5:15-16: *"Don't hide your light under a basket! Instead, put it on a stand and let it shine for all. In the same way, let your good deeds shine out for all to see, so that everyone will praise your heavenly Father."* (NLT).

Conclusion:
Observations and Reflections at 90

A Different Slogan

When writing any book, and especially this one, I never want readers to assume that I am presenting material which I have mastered. I have often said that I should be wearing a T-shirt that reads "Under Construction." That has now been revised to what I believe might be a more appropriate reading: "I'm Working On It."

Attempting to live the spirit of the law is an ongoing challenge. It is not something that one accomplishes so much as something we keep our sights on as we move in that direction.

Time is Limited

At 90, things don't look quite the same as they did in earlier years. It is more obvious than ever that each day is a gift and should be treasured for the blessing it is. The spirit of the law has much to do with a focus on the big things that really matter and a relegating of lesser things to just that category. We never really have time for the lesser to begin with – it is only an illusion that we believe we have all the time in the world. At 90, there is no time to waste on criticism, judgment, bickering, political arguments, theological hair-splitting, and other things that destroy relationships and take all the joy out of life.

My Favorite Gospel

It has always been, but now more than ever, the Gospel of John is my favorite. I know it is because of the great passages of Jesus' teaching and the marvelous images of faith they provide. We have already touched on chapter ten with Jesus as the great shepherd and the insights that speak to the source of our security and leadership in life: (John 10:2-4, 11, 14-16, BARNSTONE).

> *Whoever enters through the gate*
> *Is the shepherd of the sheep.*
> *The gatekeeper opens to him*
> *And the sheep hear his voice*
> *And he calls his own sheep by name*
> *And he leads them out.*
> *When he has put all his own outside,*
> *He goes in ahead of them and the sheep follow*
> *Because they know his voice.*
>
> *I am the good shepherd.*
> *The good shepherd lays down his life for the sheep.*
> *I am the good shepherd*
> *And I know my own and my own know me.*
> *As the father knows me and I know the father.*
> *And I lay down my life for the sheep.*
> *And I have other sheep which are not of this fold.*
> *And I must also bring them in*
> *And they will hear my voice*
> *And there will be one flock and one shepherd.*

The perfect description of the spirit of the law and being led, not driven, by the shepherd.

And then, of course, there is the knock your socks off verse in John 15:9 – *As the father has loved me, I have loved you* (BARNSTONE). I am convinced this verse is meant not only for the twelve but for all of Jesus' disciples down through the years. The depth of God's love for us through Jesus his Son needs to be a daily affirmation to keep our lives anchored in the certainty that knows no fluctuation or diminishment.

Praise and Gratitude Come First

That is one of the reasons my life is filled with more gratitude and thanksgiving. I'm convinced one of the reasons there are more calls to praise than prayer in the book of Psalms is because praise is the key that unlocks a recognition and enumeration of the good gifts of God that fill each of our days. There are many who recommend beginning our time of prayer each day by listing at least three things for which we are thankful. Even in the most difficult of times there is always something for which to express gratitude. In *The Hiding Place,* set in the literal hell of Ravensbrück, Corrie Ten Boom relates how she and her sister expressed their thanks for the multitude of fleas that kept the officers from entering their barracks at night. An extreme example? Certainly, one of the ways for maintaining sanity in a situation intended to rob life of all hope.

Faith and Courage Come in the Same Package

When I read stories like the one above, I am reminded that faith is so closely tied to courage that often you cannot separate one from the other. Life is not for the faint-hearted or for the easily discouraged. As I have gotten older, I have come to find that biographies are among my favorite and most enlightening reads. The title of David McCullough's book about people who accomplished the unthinkable and, by all normal standards, the undoable, is titled *Brave Companions*. In that book I met incredible people whose lives were filled with incredible accomplishments all the while dealing with incredible obstacles. McCullough provides this insight: "If there is a prevailing, unifying theme, I suppose it is the part courage plays."[93]

---

[93] David McCullough, *Brave Companions,* xiii.

Jesus' Great Gift of Peace

After speaking about his departure in John 14, Jesus gives two promises. One is that the comforter, the Holy Spirit, will be given to his disciples to teach and guide them. He also leaves them a parting gift:

I leave you peace. My peace I give to you.
Not as the world gives, I give to you.
Do not be shaken in your heart or frightened.
You heard what I told you. (John 14:27-28, BARNSTONE).

The word with which people usually greeted one another, *Shalom,* Jesus now uses as his word of departure. But it is more than a word, it is his gift. The gift he leaves us is the gift of peace.

In the Bible, the word *peace, shalom,* never simply means the absence of trouble. Peace means everything which makes for our highest good. The peace which the world offers us is the peace of escape, the peace which comes from the avoidance of trouble, the peace which comes from refusing to face things. The peace which Jesus offers us is the peace of conquest. It is the peace which no experience in life can ever take from us. It is the peace which no sorrow, no danger, no suffering can make less. It is the peace which is independent of outward circumstances.[94]

I will confess that in some of my many years I have often joined in with the hand wringers guild and even been a member of the poor-me club. I kept thinking that if only my circumstances were different I could do so much better. I stopped looking for the perfect church because I realized it would not be a good fit; I could never be the perfect pastor. I made every effort to live with things as they were not as I wished them to be or thought they ought to be. Part of my cure came from reading history. A current read is a series by Peter Tremayne featuring Sister Fidelma and life in seventh century

---

94 William Barclay, *The Gospel of John,* Vol. 2 (Philadelphia: The Westminster Press, 1956), 199.

Ireland.[95] Even then, life was chaotic, dangerous, and full of conflict in the Christian community. Life is life. It is challenging. It has always been and always will be.

So, when I am asked if I have achieved that perfect peace that Jesus left for us my answer is the obvious: "I'm working on it."

---

95 Peter Tremayne, *The Haunted Abbot* (London: Headline Books, 2002).

Bibliography Of Quoted Sources

Alter, Robert. *The Hebrew Bible.* New York: W. W. Norton Company, 2019.

Barclay, William. *The Letters to the Corinthians.* Philadelphia: The Westminster Press, 1956.

_____. *The Gospel of Mark:* Philadelphia: The Westminster Press, 1956.

_____. *The Gospel of John.* Philadelphia: The Westminster Press, 1956.

_____. *The Gospel of Matthew.* Philadelphia: The Westminster Press, 1958.

Barnstone, Willis. *The New Covenant.* New York: Riverhead Books, 2002.

Beaton, M. C. *The Dead Ringer.* New York: Minotaur Books, 2020.

Box, C. J. *Back of Beyond.* New York: Minotaur Books, 2022.

The Broadman Bible Commentary. Nashville: Broadman Press, 1970.

Craddock, Fred. *Luke.* Louisville: John Knox Press, 2020.

Dear, John. *The Sound of Listening.* New York: Continuum, 1999.

Douglas, J. D. *The Illustrated Bible Dictionary.* Wheaton: Inter-Varsity Press, 1980.

Ellis, Joseph E. *His Excellency.* New York: Vintage Books, 2004.

The Expositor's Bible Commentary. Grand Rapids: Zondervan, 1984.

Finch, Charles. *A Beautiful Blue Death.* New York: Minotaur Books, 2017.

Goldberg, Philip. *Roadsigns on the Spiritual Path.* Boulder, CO: Sentient Publications, 2006.

Haidt, Jonathan. *The Anxious Generation.* New York: Penguin Press, 2024.

Hare, Douglas R. A. *Matthew.* Louisville: John Knox Press, 1993.

Kissinger, Henry A., Mundie, Craig, and Schmidt, Eric. *Genesis.* New York: Little, Brown and Company, 2024.

Malliet, G. M. *The Haunted Season.* New York: Minotaur Books, 2015.

McCullough, David. *Brave Companions.* New York: Simon & Schuster Paperbacks, 1992.

Mercer Dictionary of the Bible. Macon: Mercer University Press, 1991.

Muggeridge, Malcolm. *Something Beautiful for God.* San Francisco: Harper & Row, 1971.

The New Interpreter's Bible. Nashville: Abingdon Press, 1995.

Nichols, Michael P. and Straus, Martha B. *The Lost Art of Listening.* Third Edition. New York: The Guilford Press, 2021.

O'Day, Gail R. and Peterson, David L., eds. *Theological Bible Commentary.* Louisville: Westminster John Knox Press, 2009.

Peterson, Jordan. *12 Rules for Life.* Toronto: Random House Canada, 2018.

Robertson, A. T. *Word Pictures in the New Testament.* Nashville: Broadman Press, 1930.

Ten Boom, Corrie, with Sherrill, Elizabeth and John. Grand Rapids: Chosen Books, 2006.

Tremayne, Peter. *Absolution by Murder.* London: Headline Books, 1994.

_____. *The Haunted Abbot.* London: Headline Books, 2002.

_____. *A Prayer for the Damned.* New York: St. Martin's Minotaur, 2006.

_____. *The Spider's Web.* London: Headline Books, 1997.

_____. *Valley of the Shadow.* London: Headline Books, 1998.

Wuest, Kenneth S. *Mark in the Greek New Testament.* Wm. B. Eerdmans Publishing Company, 1950.

www.ingramcontent.com/pod-product-compliance
Lightning Source LLC
LaVergne TN
LVHW041633070426
835507LV00008B/600